A-Z PETERBOROUGH

Key to Map Pages	
Large Scale City Centre	
Map Pages	6

32-48

REF

Motorway	**A1(M)**	Car Park (selected)	P
A Road	A15	Church or Chapel	†
B Road	B1091	Cycleway (selected)	
Dual Carriageway		Fire Station	■
One-way Street		Hospital	H
Traffic flow on A Roads is indicated by a heavy line on the driver's left.		House Numbers (A & B Roads only)	16 4
Road Under Construction		Information Centre	i
Opening dates are correct at the time of publication.		National Grid Reference	⁴10
Proposed Road		Police Station	▲
Restricted Access		Post Office	★
Pedestrianized Road		Road Junction Number	㊱
Track / Footpath		Safety Camera with Speed Limit	㉚
Residential Walkway		Fixed cameras and long term road works cameras. Symbols do not indicate camera direction.	
Railway		Toilet	
		without facilities for the Disabled	▽
		with facilities for the Disabled	▽
Built-up Area		Educational Establishment	▢
Local Authority Boundary		Hospital or Healthcare Building	▢
Posttown Boundary		Industrial Building	▢
Postcode Boundary (within Posttown)		Leisure or Recreational Facility	▢
Map Continuation	16 Large Scale City Centre 4	Place of Interest	▢
		Public Building	▢
		Shopping Centre or Market	▢
		Other Selected Buildings	▢

Heritage Station
Station
Level Crossing

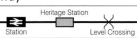

SCALE

Map Pages 6-31   1:15,840

0   ¼   ½ Mile

0   250   500   750 Metres

4 inches (10.16 cm) to 1 mile   6.31 cm to 1 km

Map Pages 4-5   1:7,920

0   ⅛   ¼ Mile

0   100   200   300   400 Metres

8 inches (20.32cm) to 1 mile   12.63 cm to 1 km

A-Z AZ AtoZ
registered trade marks of
Geographers' A-Z Map Company Ltd
www./az.co.uk

EDITION 5 2015
Copyright © Geographers' A-Z Map Co. Ltd.
Telephone: 01732 781000 (Enquiries & Trade Sales)
        01732 783422 (Retail Sales)

© Crown copyright and database rights 2015 OS 100017302.

Safety camera information supplied by www.PocketGPSWorld.com.
Speed Camera Location Database Copyright 2015 © PocketGPSWorld.com

Every possible care has been taken to ensure that, to the best of our knowledge, the information contained in this atlas is accurate at the date of publication. However, we cannot warrant that our work is entirely error free and whilst we would be grateful to learn of any inaccuracies, we do not accept responsibility for loss or damage resulting from reliance on information contained in this publication.

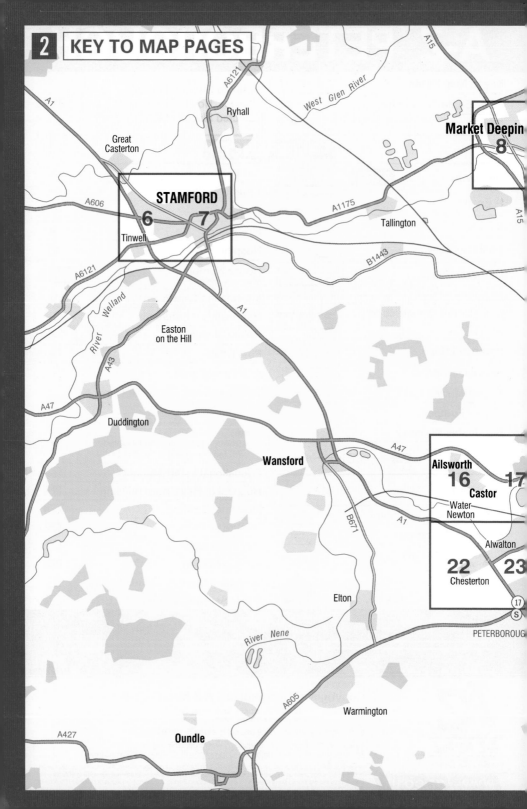

A15

A6121

West Glen River

A1

Ryhall

Market Deepin

Great
Casterton

8

A606

STAMFORD

A1175

A15

6 7

Tallington

Tinwell

A6121

B1443

River Welland

A1

Easton
on the Hill

A43

A47

Duddington

A47

Wansford

Ailsworth

16 17

Castor

Water
Newton

A1

Alwalton

B671

22 23

Chesterton

17

Elton

S

PETERBOROUG

River Nene

A427

A605

Warmington

Oundle

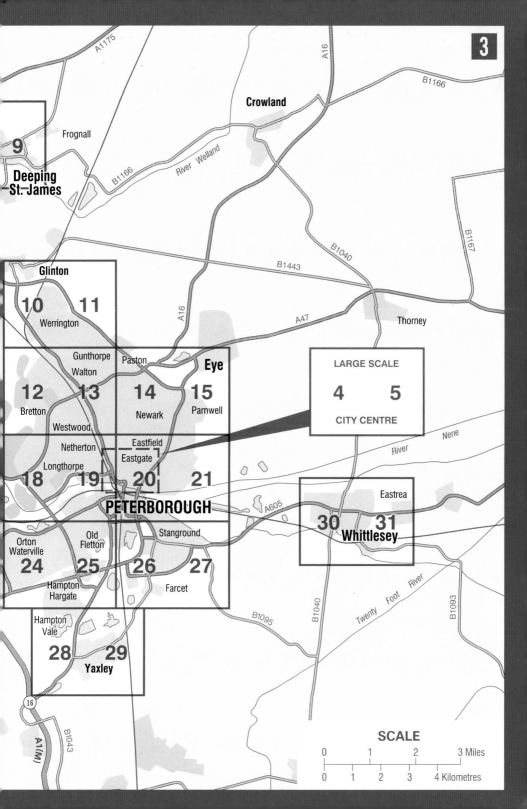

3

Frognall

Crowland

9

Deeping St. James

A1175

B1166

River Welland

B1166

A16

B1166

B1040

B1443

Glinton

10   **11**

Werrington

A16

A47

Thorney

B1167

LARGE SCALE

4   **5**

CITY CENTRE

Gunthorpe   Paston

Walton

Eye

12   **13**   **14**   **15**

Bretton

Newark   Parnwell

Westwood

Netherton   Eastfield

Longthorpe   Eastgate

18   **19**   **20**   **21**

River   Nene

PETERBOROUGH

A605

Eastrea

30   **31**

Whittlesey

Orton Waterville

Old Fletton

Stanground

24   **25**   **26**   **27**

Hampton Hargate

Farcet

B1095

B1040

Twenty   Foot   River

B1093

Hampton Vale

28   **29**

Yaxley

16

A1(M)

B1043

SCALE

0   1   2   3 Miles

0   1   2   3   4 Kilometres

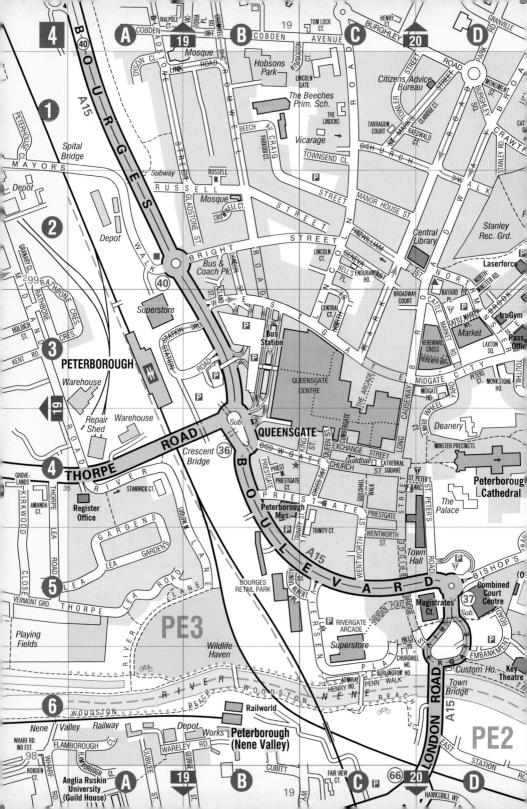

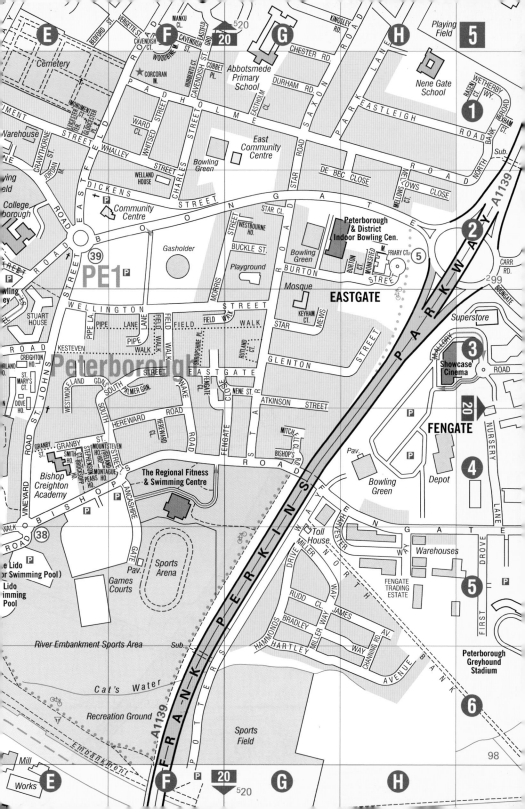

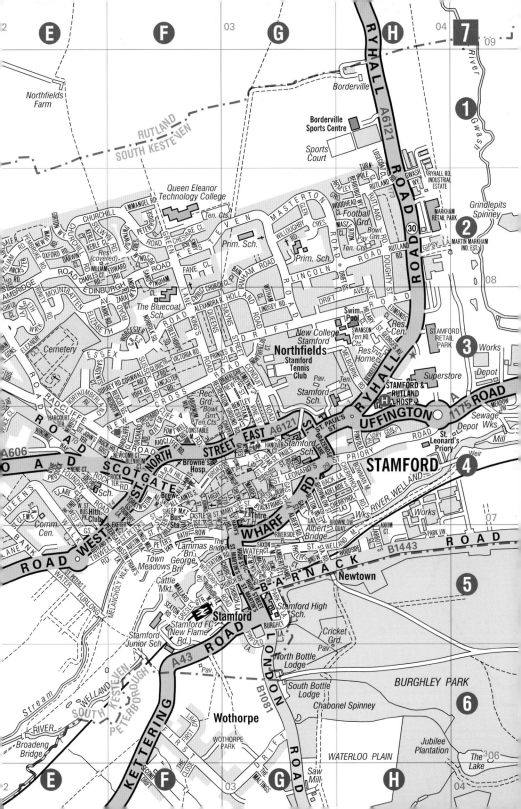

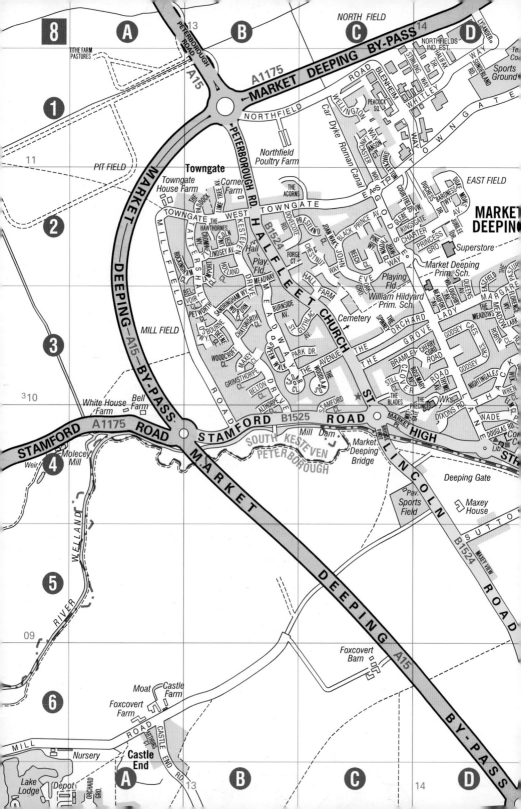

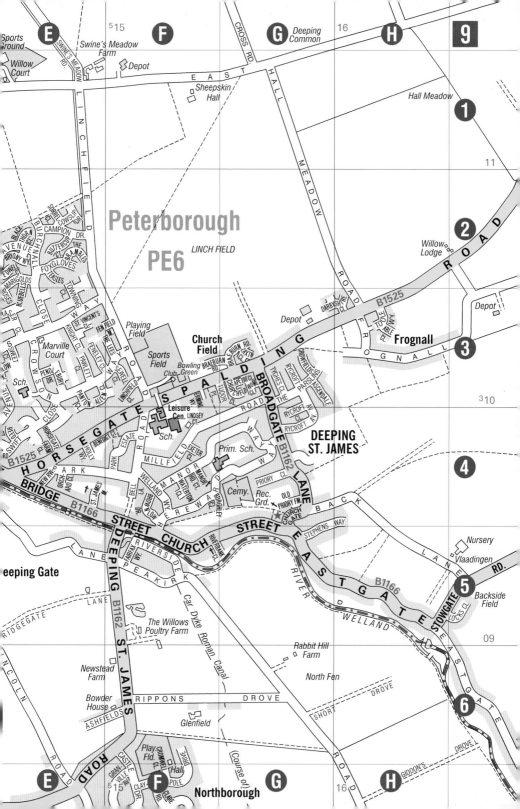

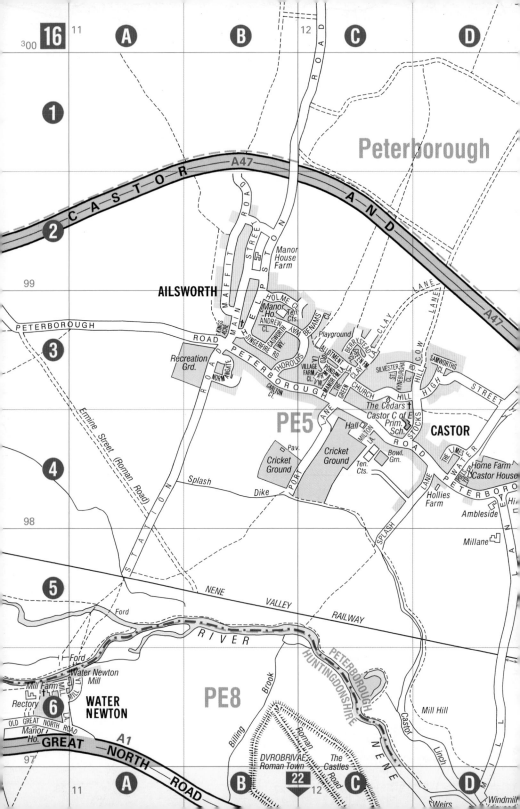

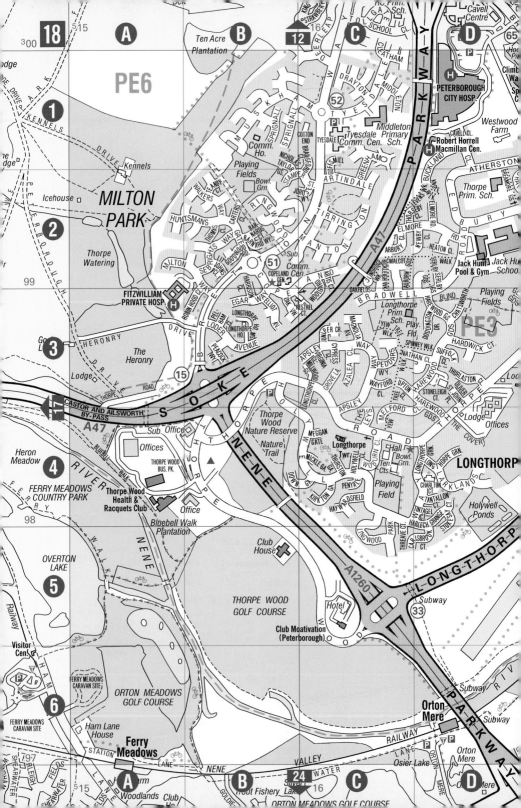

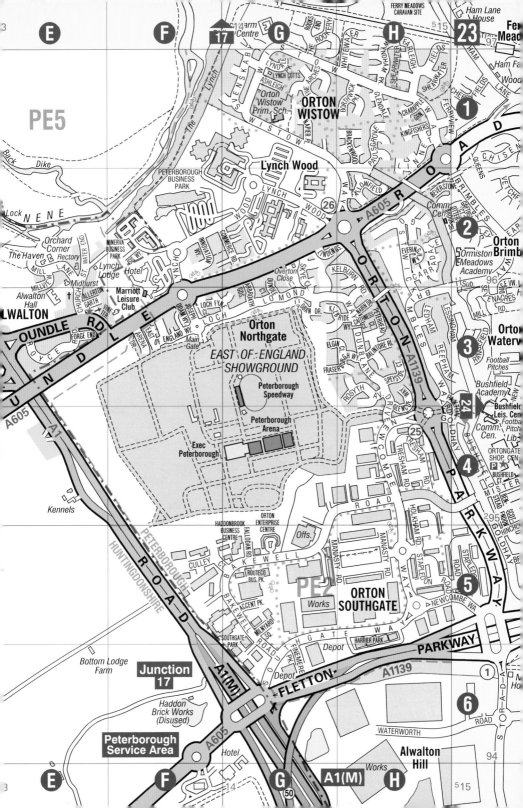

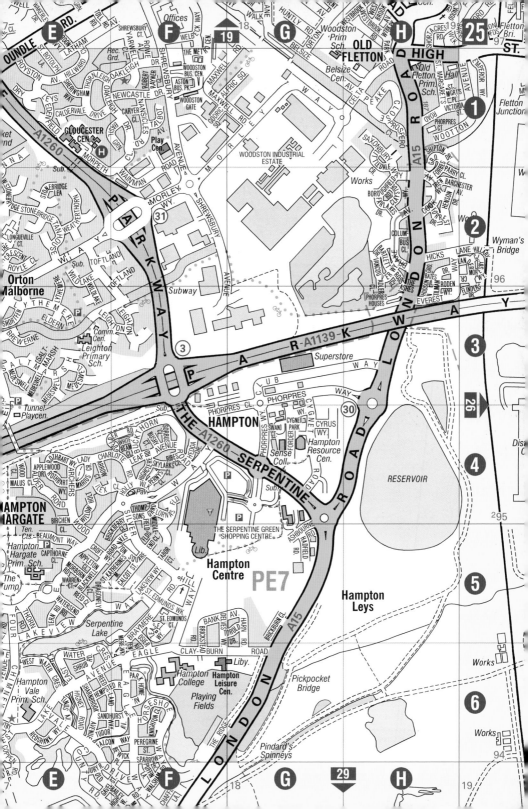

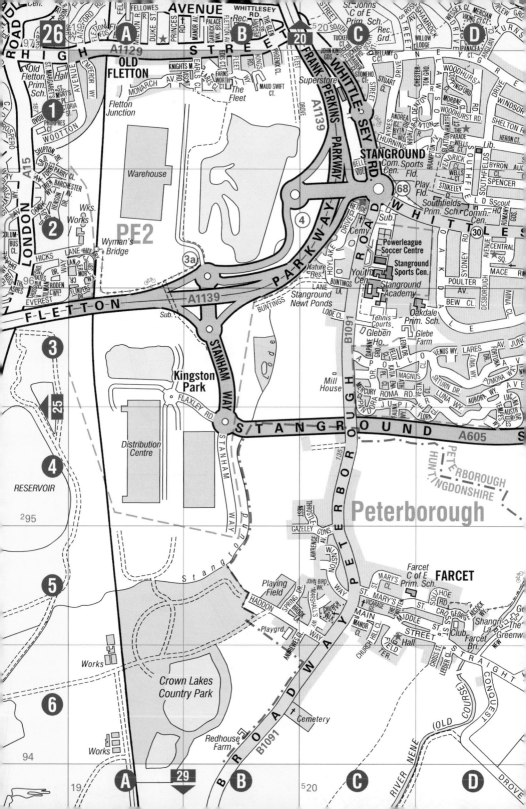

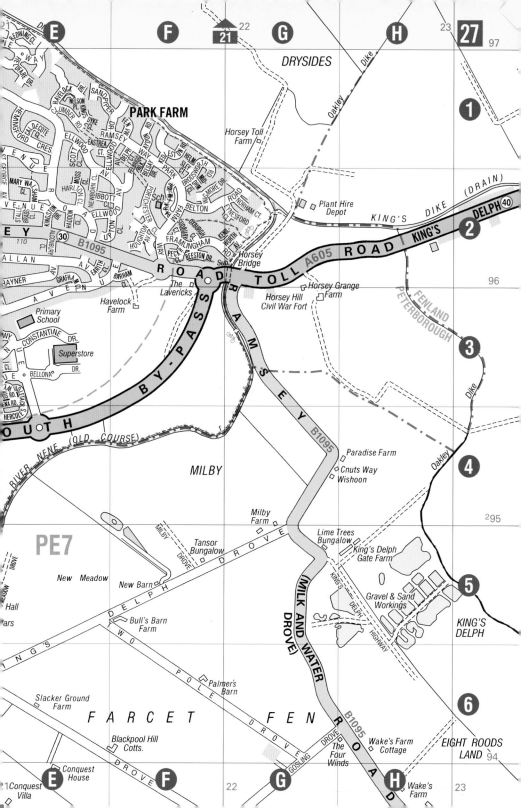

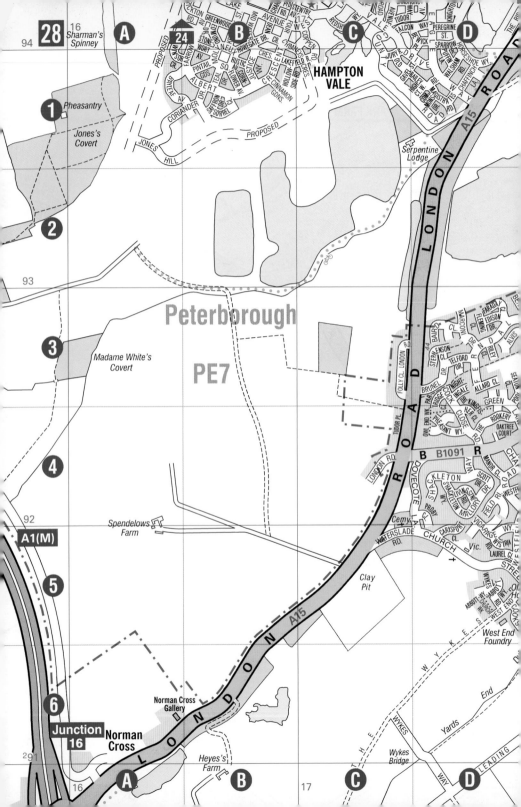

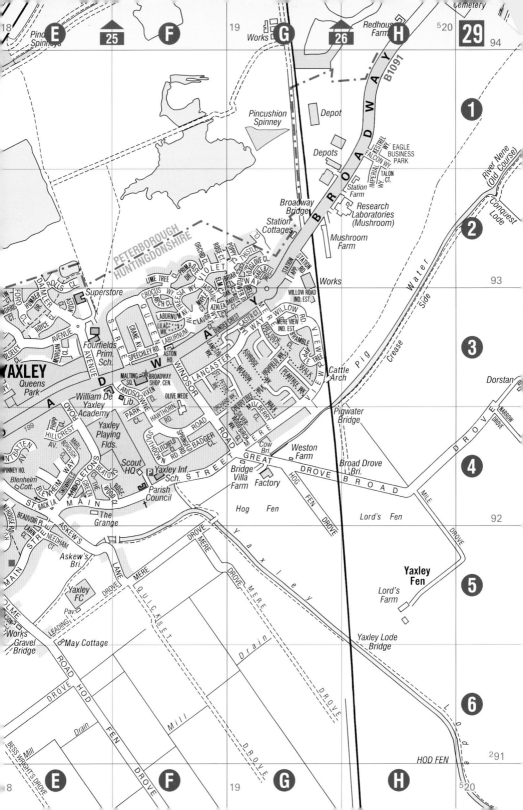

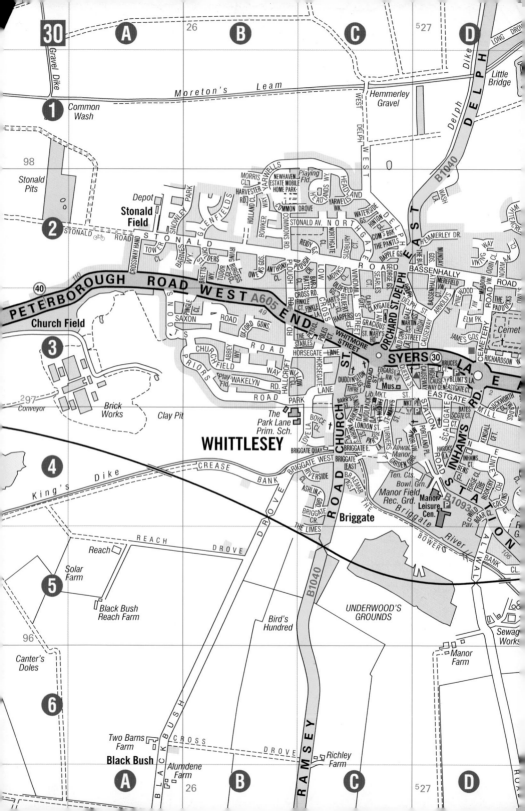

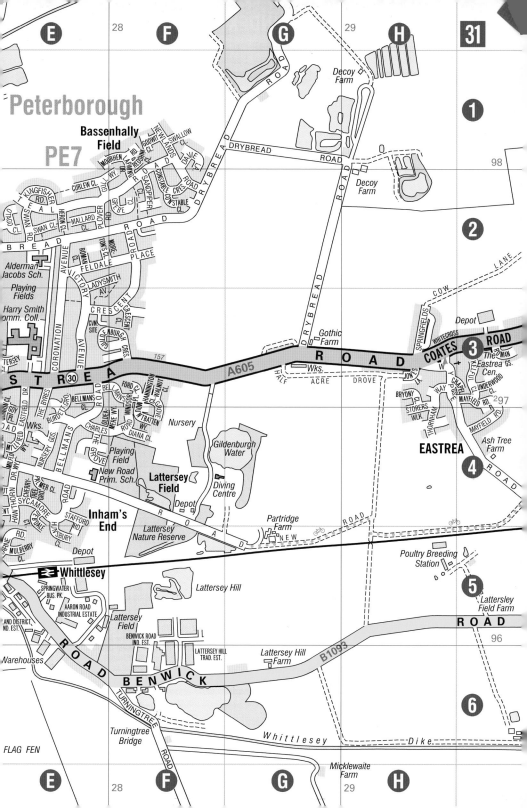

INDEX

Including Streets, Places & Areas, Hospitals etc., Industrial Estates,
Selected Flats & Walkways, Service Areas, Stations and Selected Places of Interest.

HOW TO USE THIS INDEX

1. Each street name is followed by its Postcode District, then by its Locality abbreviation(s) and then by its map reference;
e.g. **Ainsdale Dr.** PE4: Pet . . . .5D **10** is in the PE4 Postcode District and the Peterborough Locality and is to be found in square 5D on page **10**. The page number is shown in bold type.

2. A strict alphabetical order is followed in which Av., Rd., St., etc. (though abbreviated) are read in full and as part of the street name;
e.g. **Ash Rd.** appears after **Ashridge Wlk.** but before **Ashton Rd.**

3. Streets and a selection of flats and walkways that cannot be shown on the mapping, appear in the index with the thoroughfare to which
they are connected shown in brackets; e.g. **Adelaide Gdns.** *PE9: Stam . . . .4G **7** (off Adelaide St.)*

4. Addresses that are in more than one part are referred to as not continuous.

5. Places and areas are shown in the index in BLUE TYPE and the map reference is to the actual map square in which the town centre
or area is located and not to the place name shown on the map; e.g. CASTOR 3C **16**

6. An example of a selected place of interest is All Saints Brewery 4F **7**

7. Examples of stations are:
Stamford Station (Rail) . . . .5F **7**;   **Peterborough Bus Station** 3B **4** (3H **19**)

8. Service Areas are shown in the index in BOLD CAPITAL TYPE; e.g. **PETERBOROUGH SERVICE AREA** 6F **23**

9. An example of a Hospital, Hospice or selected Healthcare facility is PETERBOROUGH CITY HOSPITAL 1D **18**

10. Map references for entries that appear on large scale pages **4** & **5** are shown first, with small scale map references shown in brackets;
e.g. **Acland St.** PE1: Pet 3B **4** (2H **19**)

GENERAL ABBREVIATIONS

App. : Approach
Arc. : Arcade
Av. : Avenue
Blvd. : Boulevard
Bri. : Bridge
Bldgs. : Buildings
Bus. : Business
Cvn. : Caravan
Cen. : Centre
Cl. : Close
Cotts. : Cottages
Ct. : Court
Cres. : Crescent
Cft. : Croft
Dr. : Drive
E. : East
Ent. : Enterprise
Est. : Estate
Fld. : Field
Flds. : Fields
Gdns. : Gardens

Gth. : Garth
Ga. : Gate
Gt. : Great
Grn. : Green
Gro. : Grove
Ho. : House
Ho's. : Houses
Ind. : Industrial
Info. : Information
La. : Lane
Lit. : Little
Mnr. : Manor
Mans. : Mansions
Mkt. : Market
Mdw. : Meadow
Mdws. : Meadows
M. : Mews
Mt. : Mount
Mus. : Museum
Nth. : North

Pde. : Parade
Pk. : Park
Pas. : Passage
Pl. : Place
Ri. : Rise
Rd. : Road
Shop. : Shopping
Sth. : South
Sq. : Square
Sta. : Station
St. : Street
Ter. : Terrace
Trad. : Trading
Va. : Vale
Vw. : View
Vs. : Villas
Vis. : Visitors
Wlk. : Walk
W. : West
Yd. : Yard

LOCALITY ABBREVIATIONS

Ail : **Ailsworth**
Alw : **Alwalton**
Cas : **Castor**
Ches : **Chesterton**
Deep G : **Deeping Gate**
Deep J : **Deeping St James**
East : **Eastrea**
Elt : **Elton**
Eye : **Eye**
Far : **Farcet**
Glin : **Glinton**
Gt Cas : **Great Casterton**

Hadd : **Haddon**
Lang : **Langtoft**
Lit C : **Little Casterton**
Mar : **Marholm**
Mkt D : **Market Deeping**
Max : **Maxey**
Milk N : **Milking Nook**
Newb : **Newborough**
Nor X : **Norman Cross**
N'boro : **Northborough**
Pea : **Peakirk**

Pet : **Peterborough**
Stam : **Stamford**
Sut : **Sutton**
Tick : **Tickencote**
Tin : **Tinwell**
Uffi : **Uffington**
W New : **Water Newton**
W Deep : **West Deeping**
Whit : **Whittlesey**
Wot : **Wothorpe**
Yax : **Yaxley**

A

Aaron Rd. Ind. Est. PE7: Whit 5E **31**
Abax Stadium 5A **20**
Abbey Cl. PE6: Eye 2G **15**
Abbeyfields PE2: Pet 6A **20**
Abbey Rd. PE4: Pet 2E **13**

Abbey Way PE7: Whit 3B **30**
Abbotsbury PE2: Pet 4D **24**
Abbott's Cl. PE9: Stam 5H **7**
Abbotts Gro. PE4: Pet 3D **10**
Abbott Way PE7: Yax 5D **28**
Aberdeen Cl. PE9: Stam 3B **6**
Able Cl. PE6: Deep J 3H **9**
Aboyne Av. PE2: Pet 2B **24**

Acacia Av. PE1: Pet 3B **14**
Accent Pk. PE2: Pet 5G **23**
Acer Rd. PE1: Pet 5B **14**
Acland St. PE1: Pet 3B **4** (2H **19**)
Acorns, The PE6: Mkt D 2B **8**
Activity World 2E **21**
Adam Ct. PE1: Pet 2E **21**
Adderley PE3: Pet 4E **13**

Addington Way PE4: Pet 6E 11
Adelaide Gdns. *PE9: Stam* 4G 7
(off Adelaide St.)
Adelaide St. PE9: Stam 4G 7
Adler Cl. PE2: Pet 2H 25
Admiral Ho. PE1: Pet 6C 4 (4A 20)
AILSWORTH .3B 16
Ainsdale Dr. PE4: Pet 5D 10
Airedale Cl. PE1: Pet 5A 14
Airedale Rd. PE9: Stam 2E 7
Albany Wlk. PE2: Pet 6F 19
Alba Rd. PE7: Pet 5D 24
Albert Cres. PE7: Pet 1B 28
Albert Pl. PE1: Pet 5B 4 (4H 19)
Albert Rd. PE9: Stam 4G 7
Alconbury Cl. PE2: Pet 2E 27
Aldermans Dr. PE3: Pet 2G 19
Alder Rd. PE7: Pet 4E 25
Aldsworth Cl. PE1: Pet 5D 14
Alexandra Rd.
  PE1: Pet .5H 13
  PE9: Stam 3F 7
Alfreds Way PE4: Pet 5C 10
Alfric Sq. PE2: Pet 1G 25
Aliwal Rd. PE7: Whit 5D 30
Allan Av. PE2: Pet 2E 27
Allard Cl. PE7: Yax 3D 28
Allen Cl. PE6: Deep J 3E 9
Allen Rd. PE1: Pet 5G 13
Allerton Gth. PE7: Alw 3E 23
Allexton Gdns. PE1: Pet 4D 14
Allotment La. PE5: Cas 3C 16
All Saints Brewery 4F 7
All Saints M. PE9: Stam 4F 7
All Saints Pl. PE9: Stam 4F 7
All Saints Rd. PE1: Pet 6A 14
All Saints St. PE9: Stam 4F 7
Alma Pl. *PE9: Stam* 4F 7
(off North St.)
Alma Rd. PE1: Pet 6H 13
Almond Rd. PE1: Pet 4B 14
Almoners La. PE3: Pet 2G 19
Alnwick PE2: Pet 4C 24
Alpine Cl. PE1: Pet 4D 14
Althorpe Cl. PE6: Mkt D 4B 8
Alvis Dr. PE7: Yax 3D 28
ALWALTON .3E 23
ALWALTON HILL 6H 23
Amanda Ct. PE3: Pet 4A 4 (3G 19)
Amberley Slope PE4: Pet 6E 11
AMF Bowling
  Peterborough 4E 13
Amirs Way PE3: Pet 2G 19
Ancaster Rd. PE9: Stam 2E 7
Anchor Ct. PE4: Pet 2H 13
Andrea Cl. PE2: Pet 1C 26
Andrew Cl. PE5: Ail 3B 16
Andrewes Cl. PE7: Far 6B 26
Andrew Rd. PE9: Stam 2F 7
Andrews Cres. PE4: Pet 1H 13
Anglian Cl. PE2: Pet 1D 26
Anglia Ruskin University
  Guild House 6A 4 (5H 19)
Angus Cl. PE9: Stam 3B 6
Angus Ct. PE3: Pet 2F 19
Anne Rd. PE9: Stam 3E 7
Anson Ct. PE6: Mkt D 1C 8
Anthony Cl. PE1: Pet 3H 13
  PE7: Whit 2B 30
Apex, The PE2: Pet 5A 20
Apollo Av. PE2: Pet 5A 20
Appleton Cl. PE7: Pet 5E 25
Apple Tree Cl. PE6: Deep J 3G 9
  PE7: Yax 3G 29
Applewood Dr. PE7: Pet 4E 25
Appleyard PE7: Pet 6C 20
Apsley Way PE3: Pet 3C 18
Arbroath Gdns. PE2: Pet 3G 23
Arbury Cl. PE3: Pet 2C 18
Arcade, The PE1: Pet 3C 4 (3A 20)

Archers Wood PE7: Pet 4E 25
Arena Dr. PE2: Alw 3F 23
Argyll Way PE9: Stam 4D 6
Armley Gro. PE9: Stam 2H 7
Arnold's La. PE7: Whit 3D 30
Arnwood Cen. PE1: Pet 1F 21
Arran Rd. PE9: Stam 3B 6
Arrow Ct. PE7: Pet 4E 25
Arthur Mellows Village College
  Fitness Cen. 1A 10
Arthurs Ct. PE6: Max 6A 8
Artindale PE3: Pet 2C 18
Artis Ct. PE3: Pet 2C 18
Arundel Rd. PE4: Pet 1E 13
Ascendale PE6: Deep J 3G 9
Ascot Dr. PE1: Pet 5B 14
Ashbourne Rd. PE7: Pet 5G 25
Ashburn Cl. PE6: Glin 2B 10
Ash Cl. PE1: Pet 4C 14
Ash Ct. PE1: Pet 4C 14
Ashcroft Gdns. PE1: Pet 6C 14
Ashes, The PE7: Pet 3H 25
Ashfields PE3: Pet 3G 19
  PE6: Deep G 6E 9
Ashleigh PE2: Pet 1G 23
Ashline Gro. PE7: Whit 4C 30
Ash Pk. PE4: Pet 3D 10
Ash Pl. PE9: Stam 3B 6
Ashridge Wlk. PE7: Yax 3G 29
Ash Rd. PE1: Pet 4C 14
Ashton Rd. PE3: Pet 6D 12
Ashville Rd. PE7: Pet 5D 24
Askew's La. PE7: Yax 5E 29
Aspen Cl. PE1: Pet 4B 14
Aster Dr. PE4: Pet 6F 11
Aston Bus. Pk. PE2: Pet 1F 25
Aston Cl. PE7: Yax 3E 29
Aston Ho. PE7: Yax 3F 29
Astore Pk. PE1: Pet 2E 21
Athena Cl. PE2: Pet 3C 26
Atherstone Av. PE3: Pet 1D 18
Atkinson St. PE1: Pet 3G 5 (3C 20)
Auborn Gdns. PE3: Pet 2C 18
Aubretia Av. PE4: Pet 6F 11
Audley Ga. PE3: Pet 2D 18
Audus Pl. PE9: Stam 3C 6
Augusta Cl. PE1: Pet 5E 15
Aurora Way PE2: Pet 3D 26
Auster Rd. PE2: Pet 4D 26
Austin Cl. PE7: Yax 3E 29
Austin Friar's La. PE9: Stam 5F 7
Austin St. PE9: Stam 5F 7
Avenue, The PE6: Mkt D 3C 8
Avon Ct. PE4: Pet 1G 13
Axiom Av. PE3: Pet 1E 19
Axiom Ct. PE9: Stam 5H 7
Aydon Rd. PE2: Pet 1F 27
Ayr Cl. PE9: Stam 3C 6
Ayres Dr. PE2: Pet 1C 26
Azalea Cl. PE3: Pet 3C 18
Azalea Ct. PE7: Yax 3F 29

Balmoral Rd. PE4: Pet 3E 13
Bamber St. PE1: Pet 1H 19
Bank Av. PE7: Pet 5F 25
Bank Cl. PE7: Whit 5D 30
Banks Cres. PE9: Stam 3D 6
Bannatyne Health Club
  Peterborough 5B 10
Barber Cl. PE2: Pet 1C 26
Barbers Hill PE4: Pet 2D 10
Barchester Av. PE7: Pet 2H 25
Bardney PE2: Pet 3C 24
Barford Cl. PE2: Pet 6E 19
Barham Cl. PE2: Pet 2F 27
Barkston Dr. PE1: Pet 5B 14
Barley M. PE2: Pet 6F 19
Barnack Bus. Pk. PE1: Pet 1F 21
Barnack Rd. PE9: Stam 5G 7
Barnards Ct. PE3: Pet 2B 18
Barnard Way PE3: Pet 2B 18
Barn Cl. PE4: Pet 6D 10
Barnes Way PE4: Pet 1D 12
  PE7: Whit 2A 30
Barn Hill PE9: Stam 4F 7
Barn Hill M. *PE9: Stam* 4F 7
(off Barn Hill)
Barnoak Rd. PE6: Newb 2H 11
Barnstock PE3: Pet 4C 12
Barnwell Rd. PE9: Stam 3C 6
Baron Ct. PE4: Pet 5F 11
Baroness Way PE6: Mkt D 2D 8
Barons Way PE9: Stam 5G 7
Barratts Cl. PE7: Whit 2C 30
Barrowfield PE1: Pet 4E 15
Barr's St. PE7: Whit 3C 30
Barry Wlk. PE2: Pet 6A 20
Bartlett Dr. PE2: Pet 2H 25
Barton Cl. PE4: Pet 2H 13
Bartram Ga. PE4: Pet 2G 13
Basil Grn. PE2: Pet 1F 25
Bassenhally Ct. PE7: Whit 3D 30
Bassenhally Rd. PE7: Whit 2D 30
BASSENNALLY FIELD 1F 31
Bates Cl. PE7: Whit 4D 30
Bates La. PE7: Pet 2H 25
Bath Rd. PE6: Eye 1H 15
Bath Row PE9: Stam 5F 7
Bathurst PE2: Pet 3C 24
Baulk, The PE7: Whit 2D 30
Baxter Cl. PE4: Pet 3F 13
Bayard Pl. PE1: Pet 3D 4
Bayleaf Av. PE7: Pet 1A 28
Bayston Ct. PE2: Pet 5G 19
Beadle Way PE4: Pet 1A 14
Beatons Cl. PE7: Yax 4E 29
Beaufort St. PE1: Pet 4D 30
Beaufort Av. PE6: Mkt D 3D 8
Beaulieu Ct. PE6: Eye 1G 15
Beaumont Way PE7: Pet 5E 25
Beauvale Gdns. PE4: Pet 6G 11
Beauvoir Pl. PE7: Yax 4E 29
Beckets Cl. PE1: Pet 3H 13
Beckingham PE2: Pet 4B 24
Bede Pl. PE1: Pet 5A 14
Bedford St. PE1: Pet 1E 5 (1B 20)
Beech Av. PE1: Pet 1B 4 (2H 19)
Beech Cl. PE6: Mkt D 2C 8
Beech Gro. PE9: Stam 3B 6
Beech La. PE6: Eye 1G 15
Beech Rd. PE6: Glin 1A 10
Beechwood Cl. PE1: Pet 4C 14
Beeston Dr. PE2: Pet 2F 27
Belgic Sq. PE1: Pet 2E 21
Belgravia Ho. PE3: Pet 3G 19
Belham Rd. PE1: Pet 4G 13
Bellamy Ct. PE2: Pet 1C 26
Bell Cotts. *PE9: Stam* 4G 7
(off St Leonard's St.)
Belle Vue PE2: Pet 1C 26
Bellflower Dr. PE7: Yax 3G 29
Bell La. PE6: Deep J 4F 9
Bellmans Cl. PE7: Whit 3E 31
Bellmans Gro. PE7: Whit 3F 31

B

Back La. PE6: Deep J 4G 9
  PE6: Eye .1H 15
  PE7: Yax .4E 29
  PE9: Stam 4G 7
Bader Cl. PE3: Pet 5E 13
Badger Cl. PE7: Yax 4F 29
Badington Cl. PE2: Pet 5F 19
Bailey Way PE2: Pet 5F 19
Bain Cl. PE9: Stam 2G 7
Bainton Rd. PE6: Milk N 1H 11
Baird Cl. PE7: Yax 3D 28
Bakers La. PE7: Pet 6G 19
Bakewell Rd. PE2: Pet 5G 23
Bala Ct. PE4: Pet 6G 11
Baldwin Dr. PE2: Pet 5G 19
Balintore Ri. PE2: Pet 3H 23

Bellmans Rd. PE7: Whit 4E 31
Bellona Dr. PE2: Pet 3E 27
Bell's Pl. PE1: Pet 2C 4 (2A 20)
Belsay Dr. PE2: Pet 2F 27
Belsize Av. PE2: Pet 6G 19
Belton Cl. PE6: Mkt D 3B 8
Belton Gdns. PE9: Stam 4G 7
Belton Rd. PE2: Pet 2F 27
Belton St. PE9: Stam 4G 7
Beluga Cl. PE2: Pet 5B 20
Belvoir Cl. PE6: Mkt D 3B 8
  PE9: Stam 3C 6
Belvoir Way PE1: Pet 3C 14
Benams Cl. PE5: Cas 3C 16
Benedict Ct. PE6: Deep J 4E 9
Benedict Sq. PE4: Pet 1C 12
Benland PE3: Pet 5C 12
Bens Cl. PE7: Whit 4D 30
Benstead PE2: Pet 4A 24
Bentley Av. PE7: Yax 3D 28
Bentley St. PE9: Stam 3G 7
Benwick Rd. PE7: Whit 6F 31
Benwick Rd. Ind. Est. PE7: Whit . . .5F 31
Benyon Gro. PE2: Pet 3D 24
Berkeley Ct. PE9: Stam 3H 7
Berkeley Rd. PE3: Pet 2E 19
Berrybut Way PE9: Stam 2H 7
Berry Ct. PE1: Pet 6G 13
Berrystead PE5: Cas 3C 16
Bess Wright's Drove PE7: Yax 6E 29
Bettles Cl. PE1: Pet 5A 14
Beverley Gdns. PE9: Stam 3E 7
Beverstone PE2: Pet 2H 23
Bevishall PE4: Pet 2H 13
Bew Cl. PE2: Pet 3D 26
Bewick Pl. PE7: Pet 6F 25
Bickleigh Wlk. PE3: Pet 2C 18
Bifield PE2: Pet 4B 24
Big Sky Adventure Play Cen. 1F 25
Birch Cl. PE7: Yax 4G 29
Birchen Cl. PE7: Pet 4E 25
Birch Rd. PE9: Stam 2B 6
Birchtree Av. PE1: Pet 4A 14
Birchwood PE2: Pet 4C 24
Birkdale Av. PE4: Pet 6D 10
Bishops Cl. PE1: Pet 6D 14
Bishopsfield PE4: Pet 2F 13
Bishop's Rd. PE1: Pet 5D 4 (4A 20)
BLACK BUSH 6A 30
Blackbush Drove PE7: Whit 6A 30
Blackdown Gth. PE4: Pet 6F 11
Blackfriars St. PE9: Stam 4G 7
Blackmead PE2: Pet 3D 24
Black Path PE9: Stam 3G 7
  (off Conduit Rd.)
Black Prince Av. PE6: Mkt D 2C 8
Blackstone's Ct. PE9: Stam 3H 7
  (off St Georges Av.)
Black Swan Cres. PE7: Pet 5D 24
Blackthorn PE9: Stam 2A 6
Blackthorn Cl. PE6: Deep J 2E 9
Blackwell Rd. PE7: Pet 5E 25
Blades, The PE6: Mkt D 3C 8
Blandford Gdns. PE1: Pet 4E 15
Blashfield Cl. PE9: Stam 3E 7
Blenheim Ct. PE9: Stam 4F 7
Blenheim Way PE6: Mkt D 1C 8
  PE7: Yax 4E 29
Blind La. PE3: Pet 3D 18
Blossom Ct. PE3: Pet 3D 12
Bluebell Av. PE1: Pet 3A 14
Bluebell Rd. PE9: Stam 2B 6
Bluebells PE6: Deep J 3E 9
Bluebell Wlk. PE3: Pet 4A 18
Blunt's La. PE7: Whit 4C 30
Boardwalks Local Nature Reserve, The
  . . . . .4F 19
Bodesway PE2: Pet 3D 24
Boleyn Av. PE2: Pet 5E 19
Boongate PE1: Pet 3H 5 (2B 20)
Borderville Sports Cen. 1G 7

Boroughfield Rd. PE2: Pet 2H 25
Borrowdale Cl. PE4: Pet 6G 11
Borthwick Pk. PE2: Pet 1H 23
Boswell Cl. PE1: Pet 3G 13
Botolph Bri. Ind. Est. PE2: Pet 6F 19
Botolph Grn. PE2: Pet 6E 19
Boulevard Retail Pk., The
  PE1: Pet 4F 13
Bourges Blvd. PE1: Pet 1A 4 (4F 13)
Bourges Retail Pk. PE1: Pet . .5B 4 (4H 19)
Bowberry Cl. PE6: Eye 1H 15
Bower, The PE7: Whit 4C 30
Bower Cl. PE1: Pet 6C 14
Bowker Way PE7: Whit 2B 30
Bowman M. PE2: Stam 4H 7
Bowness Way PE4: Pet 1H 13
Boxgrove Cl. PE6: Eye 1H 15
Boyce Cl. PE7: Whit 4C 30
Bozeat Way PE3: Pet 5E 13
Brackenwood PE2: Pet 1H 23
Brackley Cl. PE3: Pet 2F 19
Bradden St. PE3: Pet 5E 13
Bradegate Dr. PE1: Pet 4E 15
Bradfield Way PE1: Pet 6A 14
Bradley Way PE1: Pet 5G 5 (4C 20)
Bradshaw Cl. PE9: Stam 3C 6
Bradwell Rd. PE3: Pet 3C 18
Braeburn PE6: Deep J 3G 9
Braemar Cl. PE9: Stam 3C 6
Braemar Gdns. PE7: Whit 4C 30
Brailsford Cl. PE3: Pet 1C 18
Bramall Cl. PE3: Pet 2D 18
Bramble Cl. PE7: Whit 4D 30
  PE7: Yax 3G 29
Bramble Gro. PE9: Stam 3B 6
Brambles, The PE6: Deep J 2E 9
Bramhall Pl. PE1: Pet 2F 21
Bramley Rd. PE6: Mkt D 3C 8
Brampton Cl. PE2: Pet 1D 26
Brancepeth Pl. PE2: Pet 5G 19
Branston Ri. PE1: Pet 4D 14
  (not continuous)
Brassey Cl. PE1: Pet 5G 13
Braybrook PE2: Pet 4C 24
Braymere Rd. PE7: Pet 5F 25
Brazenose La. PE9: Stam 4G 7
Bread St. PE2: Pet 5H 19
Breamore Gdns. PE3: Pet 2D 18
Brendon Gth. PE4: Pet 2G 13
BRETTON .5C 12
Bretton Cen. PE3: Pet 5C 12
Bretton Gate PE3: Pet 5C 12
Bretton Grn. PE3: Pet 6C 12
Bretton Ind. Area PE3: Pet 3E 13
Bretton Way PE3: Pet 6C 12
Bretts Way PE7: Whit 2B 30
Brewerne PE2: Pet 3E 25
Brewster Av. PE2: Pet 5H 19
Breydon Cen. PE1: Pet 2D 20
Briar Ct. PE7: Yax 2G 29
Briar Way PE1: Pet 6C 14
Brickberry Cl. PE7: Pet 5E 25
Brickburn Cl. PE7: Pet 5E 25
Brickenden Rd. PE4: Pet 6H 11
Brickstead Rd. PE7: Whit 5F 25
Brickton Rd. PE7: Pet 6D 24
Bridge Foot PE6: Deep G 4C 8
Bridgegate La. PE6: Deep G 5E 9
Bridgehill Rd. PE6: Newb 3G 11
Bridge St. PE1: Pet 5C 4 (3A 20)
  PE6: Deep J 4E 9
Bridle La. PE7: Pet 6D 24
BRIGGATE 4C 30
Briggate Cres. PE7: Whit 4C 30
Briggate E. PE7: Whit 4C 30
Briggate Quay PE7: Whit 4C 30
Briggate W. PE7: Whit 4B 30
Bright St. PE1: Pet 2B 4 (2H 19)
Brigstock Ct. PE3: Pet 5E 13
Brimbles Way PE2: Pet 2A 24

Bringhurst PE2: Pet 3C 24
Bristol Av. PE4: Pet 6D 10
Briton Ct. PE2: Pet 6D 20
Broad Cl. PE1: Pet 6D 14
Broad Drove PE7: Yax 4H 29
Broadgate La. PE6: Deep J 3G 9
Broadlands, The PE1: Pet 6E 15
Broad St. PE7: Whit 3C 30
  PE9: Stam 4F 7
Broadway PE1: Pet 3D 4 (3A 20)
  PE7: Far, Yax 4D 28
Broadway Ct. PE1: Pet 3C 4 (3A 20)
Broadway Gdns. PE1: Pet 6B 14
Broadway Shop. Cen. PE7: Yax 3F 29
Brocklesby Gdns. PE3: Pet 2E 19
Brocksopp Ho. PE1: Pet 4E 5
Brodsworth Rd. PE2: Pet 2F 27
Brooke Av. PE9: Stam 5C 6
Brooker Av. PE4: Pet 1A 14
Brookfield Home Pk. PE4: Pet 1C 12
Brookfield Ind. Pk. PE4: Pet 1D 12
Brookfurlong PE3: Pet 5D 12
Brook La. PE7: Far 5B 26
Brookside PE4: Pet 1F 13
Brook St. PE1: Pet 3D 4 (3A 20)
Broom Cl. PE1: Pet 3A 14
  (not continuous)
Brotherhood Cl. PE4: Pet 4F 13
Brotherhood Shop. Pk. PE4: Pet 3E 13
Brownlow Dr. PE7: Pet 4F 9
Brownlow Quay PE9: Stam 4G 7
Brownlow Rd. PE1: Pet 5A 14
Brownlow St. PE9: Stam 4G 7
Brownlow Ter. PE9: Stam 4G 7
  (off Back La.)
Bruces Ct. PE7: Whit 3D 30
Brudenell PE2: Pet 5A 24
Brunel Dr. PE7: Yax 3D 28
Brynmore PE3: Pet 3C 12
Bryony Cl. PE7: East 3H 31
Bryony Way PE6: Deep J 2E 9
Buckland Cl. PE3: Pet 2D 18
Buckles Gdns. PE7: Whit 3E 31
Buckle St. PE1: Pet 2G 5 (2C 20)
Buckminster Pl. PE1: Pet 4D 14
Buckthorn Rd. PE7: Pet 4F 25
Bugle La. PE9: Stam 4F 7
  (off Castle St.)
Bullock Rd. PE7: Hadd 6A 22
Buntings La. PE7: Far 3B 26
Burchnall Cl. PE6: Deep J 2E 9
Burdett Gro. PE7: Whit 4E 31
Burford Way PE1: Pet 5D 14
Burgess Rd. PE9: Stam 2D 6
Burghfield Grn. PE4: Pet 1A 14
Burghley Cl. PE6: Deep J 4F 9
Burghley Ct. PE9: Stam 4G 7
  (off Recreation Ground Rd.)
Burghley La. PE9: Stam 5G 7
Burghley Rd. PE1: Pet 1C 4 (1A 20)
  PE9: Stam 2E 7
Burghley Sq. PE1: Pet 1D 4 (2A 20)
Burlington Ho. PE1: Pet 6C 4 (4A 20)
Burmer Rd. PE1: Pet 4G 13
Burns Cl. PE1: Pet 4H 13
Burnside Av. PE6: Mkt D 3B 8
Burns Rd. PE9: Stam 3D 6
Burrows Ct. PE1: Pet 6A 14
Burswood PE2: Pet 5A 24
Burton Cl. PE1: Pet 2H 5 (2C 20)
Burton St. PE1: Pet 2G 5 (2C 20)
Burwell Reach PE2: Pet 6E 19
Burystead PE2: Pet 5B 20
Bushfield PE2: Pet 4A 24
Bushfield Cl. PE2: Pet 4A 24
Bushfield Leisure Cen. 4A 24
Bushy Ct. PE7: Whit 4F 25
Buttercup Cl. PE9: Stam 2B 6
Buttercup Ct. PE6: Deep J 2E 9
Buttermere Pl. PE4: Pet 6G 11
Byres, The PE7: Whit 4E 31

Byron Cl. PE2: Pet 1D 26
Byron Way PE9: Stam 4C 6
Bythorn Rd. PE2: Pet 1C 26
Bythorn Way PE2: Pet 1C 26

C

Caithness Cl. PE2: Pet 3H 23
Caithness Rd. PE9: Stam 3C 6
Calcot St. PE7: Pet 5F 25
Caldbeck Cl. PE4: Pet 1H 13
Caldecote Cl. PE2: Pet 1E 27
Caldervale PE2: Pet 1E 25
Caledonian Rd. PE9: Stam 3C 6
Cambrian Way PE4: Pet 2G 13
Cambridge Av. PE1: Pet 6H 13
Cambridge Rd. PE9: Stam 3E 7
Camelia Cl. PE4: Pet 6F 11
Campaign Av. PE2: Pet 5F 19
Campbell Dr. PE4: Pet 5G 11
Campion Dr. PE6: Deep J 2E 9
Campion Gro. PE9: Stam 2B 6
Campion Rd. PE1: Pet 3B 14
Candidus Ct. PE4: Pet 4D 10
Candy St. PE2: Pet 5G 19
Cane Av. PE2: Pet 5F 19
Canonsfield PE4: Pet 5C 10
Canterbury Rd. PE4: Pet 6D 10
Canwell PE4: Pet 5E 11
Capthorne Cl. PE7: Pet 5E 25
Cardinals Ga. PE4: Pet 5C 10
Carisbrook Ct. PE3: Pet 5C 18
Carisbrooke Gro. PE9: Stam 4C 6
Carleton Crest PE4: Pet 3F 13
Carl Hall Ct. PE1: Pet 3H 13
Carlton Ct. PE5: Cas 3B 16
Carmel Av. PE2: Pet 5G 19
Carradale PE2: Pet 2H 23
Carrier Ct. PE4: Pet 5F 19
Carron Dr. PE4: Pet 6C 10
Carr Rd. PE1: Pet 2H 5 (2D 20)
Carr Rd. Ind. Est.
    PE1: Pet 2D 20
Carters Cl. PE3: Pet 2B 18
Cartmel Way PE6: Eye 1G 15
Cartwright Gro. PE4: Pet 1A 14
Caryer Cl. PE2: Pet 1F 25
Carysfort Cl. PE7: Yax 5D 28
Casterton La. PE9: Tin 5A 6
Casterton Rd. PE9: Stam 3C 6
    (not continuous)
Castle Dr. PE6: N'boro 6F 9
Castle Dyke PE9: Stam 5F 7
CASTLE END 6A 8
Castle End Rd. PE6: Max 6A 8
Castle La. PE9: Stam 5F 7
    (off St Peter's Va.)
Castle St. PE9: Stam 4F 7
CASTOR 3C 16
Castor & Ailsworth By-Pass
    PE5: Ail, Cas 2A 16
    PE6: Cas 2A 16
Castor Rd. PE6: Mar .....3A 12 & 1F 17
Casworth Way PE5: Ail 3B 16
Cathedral Grn. PE1: Pet ..1D 4 (2A 20)
Cathedral Sq. PE1: Pet ...4C 4 (3A 20)
Catherine Cl. PE2: Pet 6D 18
Cathwaite PE4: Pet 2H 13
Catkins, The PE1: Pet 3C 14
    (off Scalford Dr.)
Catley PE4: Pet 2A 14
Cattle Mkt. Rd. PE1: Pet ..3D 4 (3A 20)
Cattle Mkt. Way PE1: Pet ..3D 4 (3A 20)
Causeway Cen. PE7: Whit 3D 30
Causeway M. PE7: Whit 3D 30
    (off High Causeway)
Cavell Cl. PE3: Pet 1D 18
Cavendish Ct. PE1: Pet 1F 5
Cavendish St. PE1: Pet ...1F 5 (1B 20)
Caverstede Rd. PE4: Pet 2F 13

Cecil Ct. PE9: Stam 4G 7
    (off Wharf Rd.)
Cecil Pacey Ct. PE1: Pet 4G 13
Cecil Rd. PE1: Pet 5A 14
Cedar Cl. PE6: Mkt D 3B 8
Cedar Gro. PE1: Pet 3B 14
Cedar Rd. PE9: Stam 3B 6
Celta Rd. PE2: Pet 1H 25
Celtic Cl. PE2: Pet 6D 20
Cemetery Rd. PE7: Whit 3D 30
Central Av. PE1: Pet 5B 14
Central Ct. PE1: Pet 3C 4
Central Pk. Cl. PE1: Pet 1C 20
Central Sq. PE2: Pet 2D 26
Century Sq. PE1: Pet 6H 13
Cerris Rd. PE1: Pet 4B 14
Chadburn PE4: Pet 2A 14
Chadburn Cen. PE4: Pet 2A 14
Chaffinch La. PE7: Pet 1D 28
Chain Cl. PE1: Pet 5B 14
Challenger Way PE1: Pet 6F 15
Chamberlain Way PE4: Pet 1B 14
Chancery La. PE6: Eye 1F 15
Chandlers PE2: Pet 2A 24
Channing Rd. PE1: Pet 6H 5 (4C 20)
Chantry Cl. PE1: Pet 6A 14
Chapel Ct. PE9: Stam 4G 7
    (off Chapel Yd.)
Chapel Gdns. PE7: East 3H 31
Chapel La. PE2: Pet 2B 24
    PE4: Pet 6E 11
Chapel St. PE1: Pet 3D 4 (3B 20)
    PE2: Pet 6C 20
    PE7: Yax 4D 28
Chapel Yd. PE9: Stam 4G 7
Charles Cope Rd. PE2: Pet 2B 24
Charles Rd. PE7: Whit 4E 31
    PE9: Stam 2E 7
Charles St. PE1: Pet 2F 5 (2B 20)
Charlock Dr. PE9: Stam 3B 6
Charlotte Way PE3: Pet 2F 19
Charlton Ct. PE3: Pet 4D 18
Charlton Cres. PE7: Pet 6D 24
Charnwood PE2: Pet 6A 20
Charter Av. PE6: Mkt D 2C 8
Chartwell Cl. PE2: Pet 5A 20
Chatsfield PE4: Pet 3C 10
Chatsworth Cl. PE6: Mkt D 3B 8
Chatsworth Pl. PE3: Pet 3D 18
Chatsworth PE9: Stam 3C 6
Chaucer Rd. PE1: Pet 4F 13
Chedworth PE4: Pet 3G 13
Chelmer Gth. PE4: Pet 3H 13
Cheltenham Cl. PE1: Pet 5B 14
Chelveston Way PE3: Pet 1E 19
Cherryfields PE2: Pet 1A 24
Cherry Gro. PE6: Mkt D 3D 8
Cherryholt La. PE9: Stam 4H 7
Cherryholt Rd. PE9: Stam 4H 7
Cherry Orton Rd. PE2: Pet 3B 24
Cherrytree Gro. PE1: Pet 5C 14
    PE7: Whit 4E 31
Cherrytree Wlk. PE7: Yax 3G 29
Cheshire Cl. PE9: Stam 2F 7
Chester Rd. PE1: Pet 1G 5 (1C 20)
CHESTERTON 4D 22
Chesterton Gro. PE2: Pet 1D 26
Chestnut Av. PE1: Pet 4B 14
Chestnut Cl. PE6: Glin 1A 10
Chestnut Cres. PE7: Whit 4D 30
Chestnut Gdns. PE9: Stam 4B 6
Chestnut Way PE6: Mkt D 2C 8
Cheviot Av. PE4: Pet 1G 13
Cheyne La. PE9: Stam 4G 7
Cheyney Ct. PE2: Pet 3D 24
Childers St. PE7: Whit 2B 30
Chiltern Ri. PE4: Pet 1F 13
Chippenham M. PE2: Pet 5E 19
Chisenhale PE2: Pet 1A 24
Christ Church Cl. PE9: Stam 3F 7
Christopher Cl. PE1: Pet 3H 13

Church Ct. PE9: Stam 5G 7
Church Dr. PE2: Pet 3B 24
CHURCH FIELD
    PE6 ....3F 9
    PE7 ....3A 30
Churchfield Cl. PE6: Deep J 3G 9
Churchfield Ct. PE4: Pet 3F 13
Churchfield Rd. PE4: Pet 2F 13
Churchfield Way PE7: Whit 3B 30
Church Ga. PE6: Deep J 4G 9
Church Hill PE5: Cas 3C 16
Church Hill Cl. PE7: Far 6C 26
Churchill Ho. PE1: Pet 6C 4
Churchill Rd. PE9: Stam 2E 7
Church La. PE2: Pet 6C 20
    (Copper Beech Way)
    PE2: Pet 6B 20
    (Fletton Av.)
    PE2: Pet 2B 24
    (Gannocks Cl.)
    PE9: Stam 5G 7
Church St. PE1: Pet 4C 4 (3A 20)
    PE2: Pet 6C 20
    PE4: Pet 6D 10
    PE6: Deep J 5F 9
    PE6: Mkt D 3C 8
    PE7: Alw 3E 23
    PE7: Whit 4C 30
    PE7: Yax 5D 28
    PE9: Stam 5G 7
Church Vw. PE2: Pet 1D 24
Church Vw. Cl. PE2: Pet 6B 20
Church Wlk. PE1: Pet 1C 4 (2A 20)
    PE7: Far 5C 26
    PE7: Yax 5D 28
Cinnamon Gdns. PE7: Pet 1B 28
Cissbury Ring PE4: Pet 1E 13
CITY CARE CENTRE 3G 19
City Rd. PE1: Pet 3D 4 (3A 20)
Clapton Cl. PE9: Stam 3C 6
Clare Cl. PE9: Stam 4E 7
Clarence Rd. PE1: Pet 6G 13
Clarendon Way PE6: Glin 1B 10
Clare Rd. PE1: Pet 5H 13
    PE6: N'boro 6F 9
Claridge Ct. PE1: Pet 1D 4
Clavering Wlk. PE4: Pet 4D 10
Clayburn Rd. PE7: Pet 6F 25
Claygate PE7: Whit 3C 30
Clay La. PE5: Cas 3C 16
Claypole Dr. PE6: N'boro 6F 9
Clayside Way PE2: Pet 2H 25
Clayton PE2: Pet 3C 24
    (not continuous)
Cleatham PE3: Pet 1C 18
Clement Dr. PE2: Pet 5F 19
Cleveland Ct. PE4: Pet 1G 13
Cleve Pl. PE6: Eye 1G 15
Cliff Cres. PE9: Stam 4F 7
Cliff Rd. PE9: Stam 4F 7
Clifton Av. PE3: Pet 2G 19
Clipston Wlk. PE3: Pet 6F 13
Cloisters, The PE6: Eye 2G 15
Close, The PE9: Stam 3H 7
    (off Melbourne Rd.)
    PE9: Wot 6F 7
Clover Ct. PE7: Yax 2G 29
Clover Gdns. PE9: Stam 3A 6
Clover Rd. PE6: Mkt D 3C 8
Club Moativation
    Peterborough 5B 18
Club Way PE7: Pet 3G 25
Clumber Rd. PE2: Pet 1E 27
Coalville Cotts. PE9: Stam 3G 7
    (off Trafalgar Ter.)
Coates Rd. PE7: East 3H 31
Cobbet Pl. PE1: Pet 1F 5
Cobden Av. PE1: Pet 1B 4 (1H 19)
Cobden St. PE1: Pet 1A 4 (1H 19)
Cock Cl. Rd. PE7: Yax 3D 28
Coleridge Pl. PE1: Pet 4G 13

College Pk. PE1: Pet 6C **14**
Collingham PE2: Pet 4B **24**
Collins Av. PE9: Stam 3D **6**
Collins Ct. PE7: Whit 4D **30**
Coltsfoot Dr. PE2: Pet 6G **19**
Columbus Cl. PE2: Pet 2H **25**
Colwyn Av. PE1: Pet 5E **15**
Combined Court Cen.
 Peterborough 5D **4** (4A **20**)
Commerce Rd. PE2: Pet 2G **23**
Common Drove PE7: Whit 2B **30**
Commons Dr. PE7: Pet 1D **28**
Commons Rd. PE7: Whit 2B **30**
Compton's Brook PE7: Whit 2C **30**
Conduit Rd. PE9: Stam 3G **7**
Coneygree Rd. PE2: Pet 1C **26**
Conifers, The PE2: Pet 1B **24**
Coningsby Rd. PE3: Pet 1C **12**
Coniston Rd. PE4: Pet 1G **13**
Connaught M. PE1: Pet 3G **13**
Conquest Drove PE7: Far 6D **26**
Constable Cl. PE7: Whit 2F **31**
Constable Cres. PE7: Whit 2F **31**
Constable M. PE9: Stam 4F **7**
Constantine Dr. PE2: Pet 3E **27**
Conway Av. PE4: Pet 1E **13**
Conworth Cl. PE1: Pet 6D **14**
Cook Av. PE7: Pet 2H **25**
Cookson Cl. PE7: Yax 5D **28**
Cookson Wlk. PE7: Yax 5E **29**
Cooper Rd. PE4: Pet 1A **14**
Copeland PE3: Pet 2B **18**
Copeland Cen. PE3: Pet 2B **18**
Coppen Rd. PE7: Pet 6E **25**
Copper Beech Way PE2: Pet 6B **20**
Coppingford Cl. PE2: Pet 1D **26**
Copsewood PE4: Pet 5E **11**
Corcoran M. PE1: Pet 1F **5**
Corfe Av. PE4: Pet 1E **13**
Coriander Dr. PE7: Pet 1B **28**
Cornflower Av. PE7: Pet 1B **28**
Cornflower Cl. PE9: Stam 3A **6**
Cornstall Bldgs. PE9: Stam 4G **7**
Cornwall Rd. PE9: Stam 3F **7**
Coronation Av. PE7: Whit 3E **31**
Cosgrove Cl. PE3: Pet 5E **13**
Cotswold Cl. PE4: Pet 2G **13**
Cottesmore Cl. PE3: Pet 1E **19**
Cottesmore Rd. PE9: Stam 4C **6**
Cotton End PE3: Pet 1C **18**
Council St. PE4: Pet 3F **13**
County Rd. PE7: Pet 6E **25**
Courtfields PE6: Mkt D 2C **8**
Courtyard, The *PE4: Pet* *6E 11*
 (off The Green)
 PE6: Deep J 4D **8**
 PE9: Stam 3E **7**
Coventry Cl. PE4: Pet 6D **10**
Coverdale Wlk. PE4: Pet 4C **10**
 (not continuous)
Covert, The PE3: Pet 4D **18**
Cowgate PE1: Pet 4B **4** (3H **19**)
Cow La. PE5: Cas 3D **16**
Cowper Rd. PE1: Pet 4H **13**
Cowslip Dr. PE6: Deep J 2E **9**
Cow Way PE7: East 3H **31**
Crabapple Grn. PE2: Pet 1H **23**
Crabtree PE4: Pet 4E **11**
Craig St. PE1: Pet 1B **4** (2H **19**)
Crane Av. PE7: Yax 3F **29**
Cranemore PE4: Pet 5C **10**
Cranford Dr. PE3: Pet 1E **19**
Crawthorne Rd. PE1: Pet 1D **4** (2A **20**)
Crawthorne St. PE1: Pet 1E **5** (2B **20**)
Crease Bank PE7: Whit 4B **30**
Creighton Ho. PE1: Pet 3E **5**
Crescent, The PE2: Pet 2E **25**
 (Royle Cl.)
 PE2: Pet 6G **19**
 (The Dell)
 PE6: Eye 1H **15**

Crescent Cl. PE7: Whit 3F **31**
Crescent Rd. PE7: Whit 3E **31**
Crescent Rd. Cvn. Site PE7: Whit . . .3E **31**
Cresset, The 6C **12**
Crester Dr. PE4: Pet 6E **11**
Crocus Gro. PE1: Pet 3A **14**
Crocus Way PE7: Yax 3F **29**
Croft, The *PE9: Stam* *4H 7*
 (off Cherryholt Rd.)
Croft Way PE7: Pet 5E **25**
Cromarty Rd. PE9: Stam 3C **6**
Cromwell Cl. PE6: N'boro 6F **9**
Cromwell Ct. PE1: Pet 2B **4** (2H **19**)
Cromwell Rd. PE1: Pet 1B **4** (1H **19**)
 (not continuous)
Cromwell Way PE6: Mkt D 2B **8**
Cropston Rd. PE1: Pet 4E **15**
Cross Drove PE7: Whit 6B **30**
Cross Keys PE1: Pet 4E **15**
Cross Keys La. PE9: Stam 4F **7**
Cross Rd. PE6: Mkt D 1G **9**
 PE7: Whit 3C **30**
Cross St. PE1: Pet 4C **4** (3A **20**)
 PE7: Far 5D **26**
Crossway Hand PE7: Whit 2A **30**
Crowfields PE6: Deep J 3G **9**
Crowhurst PE4: Pet 4E **11**
Crowland Rd. PE6: Eye 1H **15**
Crown Lakes Country Pk. 6A **26**
Crown La. PE9: Tin 6B **6**
Crown St. PE1: Pet 4G **13**
 PE9: Stam *4F 7*
 (off Broad St.)
Crowson Way PE6: Deep J 3E **9**
Croyland Rd. PE4: Pet 2F **13**
Crystal Dr. PE2: Pet 5F **19**
Cubitt Way PE2: Pet 6B **4** (5H **19**)
Culley Ct. PE2: Pet 5F **23**
Cumbergate PE1: Pet 4C **4** (3A **20**)
Cumberland Ho. PE1: Pet 3E **5**
Cunningham Rd. PE2: Pet 5G **19**
Curlew Cl. PE7: Whit 2E **31**
Curlew Gro. PE2: Pet 6D **20**
Curlew Wlk. PE6: Deep J 3D **8**
Cygnet Pk. PE7: Pet 4G **25**
Cygnet Rd. PE7: Pet 4G **25**
Cypress Cl. PE3: Pet 3C **18**
Cyrus Way PE7: Pet 4G **25**

D

Daffodil Ct. PE7: Yax 3G **29**
Daffodil Gro. PE2: Pet 6C **20**
Daimler Av. PE7: Yax 2E **29**
Daisy Dr. PE7: Pet 6D **24**
Dalby Ct. PE1: Pet 3C **14**
Dale Cl. PE2: Pet 2B **24**
Danegeld Pl. PE9: Stam 4G **7**
Danes Cl. PE1: Pet 1C **20**
Daniel Cl. PE9: Stam 5G **7**
Danish Cl. PE4: Pet 5C **10**
Daphne Gro. PE2: Pet 3C **26**
Dapple Gdns. PE7: Whit 2C **30**
Darbyshire Cl. PE6: Deep J 3G **9**
Darwin Cl. PE9: Stam 2E **7**
David Chalmers Cl. PE2: Pet 5H **19**
David's Cl. PE4: Pet 5B **10**
David's La. PE4: Pet 5C **10**
Davie La. PE7: Whit 1F **31**
Daymond St. PE2: Pet 5F **19**
Deaconscroft PE3: Pet 6D **12**
Deacon St. PE1: Pet 2B **4** (2H **19**)
Dean Cres. PE7: Pet 6D **24**
Dean's Ct. PE1: Pet 4D **4** (3A **20**)
Debdale PE2: Pet 3A **24**
De Bec Cl. PE1: Pet 2G **5** (2C **20**)
Deene Cl. PE6: Mkt D 3B **8**
Deene Ct. PE3: Pet 6E **13**
DEEPING GATE 5E **9**

DEEPING ST JAMES 4G **9**
Deeping St James Rd.
 PE6: Deep G, N'boro 5F **9**
Deepings Leisure Cen. 4F **9**
Deerhurst Way PE6: Eye 1H **15**
Deerleap PE3: Pet 6C **12**
Deer Valley Rd. PE2: Pet 5G **19**
Delamere Cl. PE1: Pet 6C **14**
Delapre Ct. PE6: Eye 1G **15**
Dell, The PE2: Pet 6G **19**
Delph PE7: Whit 2C **30**
Delph Ct. PE2: Pet 1F **27**
Delph St. PE7: Whit 3C **30**
Delves Way PE7: Pet 5F **25**
De Montfort Ct. PE2: Pet 5H **19**
Denham Wlk. PE3: Pet 1E **19**
Denis Dr. PE2: Pet 3C **24**
Denmark Dr. PE2: Pet 3C **24**
Denton Rd. PE2: Pet 1D **26**
Derby Dr. PE1: Pet 5C **14**
Derwent Dr. PE4: Pet 1G **13**
Derwood Gro. PE4: Pet 4D **10**
Desborough Av. PE2: Pet 3D **26**
Diana Cl. PE7: Whit 4F **31**
Dickens Dr. PE9: Stam 4C **6**
Dickens St. PE1: Pet 2E **5** (2B **20**)
Dingley Ct. PE3: Pet 6E **13**
Dixons Rd. PE6: Mkt D 4D **8**
Doddington Dr. PE3: Pet 3D **18**
Dodson Way PE1: Pet 3F **21**
DOGSTHORPE 4B **14**
Dogsthorpe Gro. PE1: Pet 6A **14**
Dogsthorpe Rd. PE1: Pet 4A **14**
Dogsthorpe Star Pit
 & Little Wood Nature Reserve
 . . . . .1E **15**
Donaldson Dr. PE4: Pet 1H **13**
Donegal Cl. PE4: Pet 1F **13**
Dorchester Cres. PE1: Pet 4D **14**
Doughty St. PE9: Stam 2H **7**
Douglas Rd. PE6: Mkt D 4D **8**
Dovecote Cl. PE1: Pet 4A **14**
Dovecote La. PE7: Yax 4D **28**
Dovecote Rd. PE6: Mkt D 2B **8**
Dove Gdns. PE2: Pet 5G **19**
Dove Ho. PE1: Pet 3E **5**
Dover Rd. PE4: Pet 1E **13**
Down Ga. PE3: Pet 4B **18**
Downing Cres. PE9: Stam 2F **7**
Dragonfly Cl. PE7: Pet 5E **25**
Drain Rd. PE6: Newb 3H **11**
Drake Av. PE2: Pet 2H **25**
Drayton PE3: Pet 1C **18**
Driffield Way PE7: Pet 5F **19**
Drift Av. PE9: Stam 3G **7**
Drift Gdns. PE9: Stam 2H **7**
Drift Rd. PE9: Stam 3G **7**
Drive, The PE3: Pet 3G **19**
Droveway, The PE6: Pet 2H **21**
Drybread Rd.
 PE7: East, Whit 2F **31**
 PE7: Whit 2E **31**
Dryden Rd. PE1: Pet 4G **13**
Dry Leys PE2: Pet 1E **25**
Duchess Dr. PE6: Mkt D 2D **8**
Duckworth Cl. PE7: Whit 3D **30**
Dudley Av. PE4: Pet 1E **13**
Duddington Gdns. PE7: Whit 3C **30**
Duke Mdws. PE6: Mkt D 2D **8**
Dukesmead PE4: Pet 1C **12**
Dukesmead Ind. Est. PE4: Pet 1C **12**
Dukesmead Mobile Home Pk.
 PE4: Pet 1C **12**
Duke St. PE2: Pet 6A **20**
Dukes Way PE7: Pet 6D **24**
Dunblane Dr. PE2: Pet 3H **23**
Duncombes Yd. PE9: Stam 5G **7**
Dundee Ct. PE2: Pet 2G **23**
Dundee Crest PE7: Yax 3F **29**
Dundee Dr. PE9: Stam 3C **6**
Dunsberry PE3: Pet 3B **12**

Dunstan Ct.—Forge End

Dunstan Ct. PE1: Pet 6C **14**
Durham Rd. PE1: Pet 1G **5** (2C **20**)
Dyson Cl. PE1: Pet 1A **4** (2H **19**)

E

Eagle Bus. Pk. PE7: Yax 1H **29**
Eaglesthorpe PE1: Pet 4G **13**
Eagle Way PE7: Pet 6F **25**
Eames Gdns. PE1: Pet 5E **15**
Earith Cl. PE2: Pet 2E **27**
Earls Cl. PE2: Pet 1B **26**
Earl Spencer Ct. PE2: Pet 5G **19**
Earlswood PE2: Pet 2A **24**
Easby Ri. PE6: Eye 1H **15**
East Delph PE7: Whit 2D **30**
Eastern Av. PE1: Pet 3B **14**
Eastern Cl. PE1: Pet 4D **14**
EASTFIELD 1C 20
Eastfield PE6: Mkt D 2D **8**
Eastfield Dr. PE7: Whit 4E **31**
Eastfield Gro. PE1: Pet 1F **5** (1B **20**)
Eastfield Rd. PE1: Pet 2E **5** (2B **20**)
EASTGATE 3G 5 (2C 20)
Eastgate PE1: Pet 3F **5** (3B **20**)
PE6: Deep J 5G **9**
PE7: Whit .3D **30**
Eastgate Ct. PE7: Whit 3D **30**
Eastgate M. *PE7: Whit* *3D **30***
(off Eastgate)
Eastholm Cl. PE1: Pet 1G **5** (2C **20**)
Eastlands M. PE1: Pet 5D **14**
Eastleigh Rd. PE1: Pet 1H **5** (2C **20**)
East of England Showground 3G 23
East of England Way PE2: Pet 3F **23**
EASTREA 3H 31
Eastrea Ct. PE2: Pet 1E **27**
Eastrea Rd. PE7: East, Whit 3D **30**
East Sta. Rd. PE2: Pet 6D **4** (4A **20**)
East St. PE9: Stam 4G **7**
E. Water Cres. PE7: Pet 6E **25**
Eathwaite Grn. PE4: Pet 2G **13**
Edenfield PE2: Pet 1E **25**
Edgars Row PE7: Whit 3C **30**
Edgcote Cl. PE3: Pet 6E **13**
Edgerley Bus. Pk. PE1: Pet 6F **15**
Edgerley Drain Rd. PE1: Pet 5F **15**
Edgerley Drove PE6: Eye 2F **15**
Edinburgh Av. PE4: Pet 6D **10**
Edinburgh Rd. PE9: Stam 3E **7**
Edis Ct. PE2: Pet 1B **26**
Edison Dr. PE7: Yax 3D **28**
Edmonds Cl. PE9: Stam 3H **7**
Edmund Dr. PE7: Pet 6D **24**
Edwalton Av. PE3: Pet 2G **19**
Edward Rd. PE9: Stam 2F **7**
Egar Way PE3: Pet 3B **18**
Eight Acres PE9: Stam 4E **7**
Elborne Way PE1: Pet 5E **15**
Elderflower Way PE7: Pet 6D **24**
Eldern PE2: Pet 3E **25**
Eleanor Cl. PE9: Stam 3E **7**
Elena Rd. PE2: Pet 3E **27**
Elgar Way PE9: Stam 3D **6**
Elizabeth Ct. PE1: Pet 6A **14**
Elizabeth Rd. PE9: Stam 3E **7**
Ellindon PE3: Pet 4E **13**
Elliot Av. PE3: Pet 3B **18**
Ellwood Av. PE2: Pet 1E **27**
Elm Cl. PE6: Mkt D 3D **8**
PE7: Yax 2F **29**
Elm Cres. PE6: Glin 1A **10**
Elmfield Rd. PE1: Pet 4A **14**
Elmore Rd. PE3: Pet 2C **18**
Elm Pk. PE7: Whit 3D **30**
Elm St. PE2: Pet 6H **19**
PE9: Stam .4G **7**
Elstone PE2: Pet 3C **24**
Elter Wlk. PE4: Pet 6G **11**
Elton Cl. PE9: Stam 3D **6**
Elton Furze Golf Course 6A 22
Ely Cl. PE4: Pet 6D **10**
Embankment Rd. PE1: Pet 6D **4** (4A **20**)
Emlyns Gdns. PE9: Stam 3G **7**
Emlyns St. PE9: Stam 3G **7**
Emmanuel Rd. PE9: Stam 2F **7**
Emperor Way PE2: Pet 1A **26**
Empingham Rd. PE9: Stam, Tin 3A **6**
Empson Rd. PE1: Pet 6F **15**
Endurance Ho. PE1: Pet 2C **4**
Enfield Gdns. PE3: Pet 1E **19**
(not continuous)
Engaine PE2: Pet 2D **24**
English St. PE1: Pet 6G **13**
Ennerdale Ri. PE4: Pet 1F **13**
Enterprise Way PE3: Pet 3D **12**
Ermine Cl. PE9: Stam 4D **6**
Ermine Way PE6: Deep J 3F **9**
PE9: Stam .4D **6**
Eskdale Cl. PE4: Pet 6G **11**
Essendyke PE3: Pet 4C **12**
Essex Rd. PE9: Stam 3E **7**
Everdon Way PE3: Pet 6E **13**
Everest Way PE7: Pet 3H **25**
Evergreen Dr. PE7: Pet 5D **24**
Everingham PE2: Pet 2H **23**
Exchange St. PE1: Pet 4C **4** (3A **20**)
Exec Peterborough 4F 23
Exeter Cl. PE6: Deep J 4F **9**
Exeter Ct. PE9: Stam 4F **7**
Exeter Gdns. PE9: Stam 5D **6**
Exeter Rd. PE1: Pet 5H **13**
Exton Cl. PE9: Stam 4C **6**
EYE 1H 15
Eyebrook Gdns. PE4: Pet 6G **11**
Eyebury Rd. PE6: Eye 1H **15**
Eye By-Pass PE6: Eye, Pet 2C **14**
Eye Rd. PE1: Pet 5E **15**
Eynesford Cl. PE2: Pet 2G **27**
Eyrescroft PE3: Pet 4C **12**

F

Fairchild Way PE1: Pet 4A **14**
Fairfax Way PE6: Deep G 5F **9**
Fairfield Rd. PE2: Pet 5A **20**
Fairmead Way PE3: Pet 3G **19**
Fair Vw. Ct. PE2: Pet 6C **4** (4A **20**)
Fairweather Ct. PE1: Pet 2E **21**
Falcon La. PE7: Whit 3C **30**
Falcon Way PE7: Pet 6E **25**
PE7: Yax 1H **29**
Falkirk Cl. PE9: Stam 3C **6**
Fallodan Rd. PE2: Pet 5G **23**
Fallowfield PE2: Pet 2H **23**
Fane Cl. PE9: Stam 2F **7**
Fane Rd. PE4: Pet 3G **13**
Faraday Cl. PE7: Yax 3D **28**
FARCET 5C 26
Farlakes Dr. PE2: Pet 2H **25**
Farleigh Flds. PE2: Pet 6H **17**
Farm Vw. PE5: Cas 3C **16**
Farnsworth Ct. PE2: Pet 1B **26**
Far Pasture PE4: Pet 4D **10**
Farriers Ct. PE2: Pet 6F **19**
Farringdon Cl. PE1: Pet 5D **14**
Farrow Av. PE7: Pet 1B **28**
Farthingstones PE6: Glin 1A **10**
Fauna Way PE2: Pet 4C **26**
Fawsley Gth. PE3: Pet 5E **13**
Felbrigg Wlk. PE2: Pet 1F **27**
Feldale Pl. PE7: Whit 2E **31**
Felix Cl. PE2: Pet 3C **26**
Fellowes Gdns. PE2: Pet 6A **20**
Fellowes Rd. PE2: Pet 6A **20**
Fenbridge Rd. PE4: Pet 5E **11**
Feneley Cl. PE6: Deep J 3E **9**
Fen Fld. M. PE6: Deep J 3E **9**
FENGATE 4H 5 (3D 20)
Fengate PE1: Pet 4G **5** (3C **20**)
Fengate Cl. PE1: Pet 4G **5** (3C **20**)
(not continuous)
Fengate Mobile Home Pk.
PE1: Pet 4E **21**
Fengate Trad. Est. PE1: Pet . . .5H **5** (4C **20**)
Fenlake Bus. Cen. PE1: Pet 3E **21**
Fenland Ct. *PE7: Whit* *3C **30***
(off West End)
Fenland District Ind. Est.
PE7: Whit .5E **31**
Fenmere Wlk. PE7: Pet 6F **25**
Fen Vw. PE2: Pet 1F **27**
Ferndale PE7: Yax 3D **28**
Ferndale Way PE1: Pet 2B **14**
Ferry Dr. PE6: Mar 3G **17**
Ferry Mdws. Cvn. Site PE2: Pet 6H **17**
(not continuous)
Ferry Meadows Country Pk. 5H 17
Ferry Meadows Country Pk. Vis. Cen.
. . . . .5H 17
Ferry Meadows Station
Nene Valley Railway 6A 18
Ferryview PE2: Pet 1H **23**
Ferry Wlk. PE2: Pet 4H **17**
Festival Ct. PE3: Pet 6D **12**
Fieldfare Dr. PE2: Pet 1E **27**
Field Ri. PE7: Yax 4D **28**
Fields End Cl. PE7: Pet 5F **25**
Field Ter. PE7: Far 5C **26**
Field Wlk. PE1: Pet 3F **5** (3B **20**)
(not continuous)
Fife Cl. PE9: Stam 3B **6**
Figtree Wlk. PE1: Pet 4A **14**
Finchfield PE1: Pet 4E **15**
Finchley Grn. PE3: Pet 1G **19**
Finemere Pk. PE2: Pet 6G **23**
Finkle Ct. PE7: Whit 3C **30**
Finkle La. PE7: Whit 3C **30**
Fir Rd. PE9: Stam 2B **6**
First Drift PE9: Wot 6F **7**
First Drove PE1: Pet 5H **5** (4D **20**)
Fitness First
Peterborough 1G 19
FITZWILLIAM PRIVATE HOSPITAL . . .3A 18
Fitzwilliam Rd. PE9: Stam 2E **7**
Fitzwilliam St. PE1: Pet 2C **4** (2A **20**)
Five Arches PE2: Pet 1G **23**
Flag Bus. Exchange PE1: Pet 2E **21**
Flag Fen Archaeology Pk. 3H 21
Flag Fen Heritage Cen. 2H 21
Flag Fen Mus. 3G 21
Flag Fen Rd. PE1: Pet 1C **20**
Flamborough Cl. PE2: Pet 6A **4** (4G **19**)
Flats, The PE4: Pet 2G **13**
Flaxland PE3: Pet 5C **12**
Flaxley Rd. PE2: Far 3B **26**
Fleet Drove PE2: Pet 1B **26**
Fleet Way PE2: Pet 1B **26**
Fleetwood Cres. PE1: Pet 1C **20**
Fleming Cl. PE7: Yax 3D **28**
Fleming Ct. PE2: Pet 5F **19**
Fletcher Way PE4: Pet 1A **14**
Fletton Av. PE2: Pet 5A **20**
Fletton Flds. PE2: Pet 6A **20**
Fletton Parkway PE2: Pet 6G **23**
PE7: Pet 3H **25**
Flinders Dr. PE7: Pet 3A **26**
Flora Cl. PE2: Pet 4D **26**
Flore Cl. PE3: Pet 6E **13**
Florence Cl. PE7: Whit 4E **31**
Florence Way PE6: Mkt D 3D **8**
Folly Cl. PE7: Yax 3C **28**
Fontwell Gdns. PE9: Stam 4F **7**
Forbes Dr. PE7: Pet 2H **25**
Ford Cl. PE7: Whit 3F **31**
PE7: Yax 3E **29**
Forder Way PE7: Pet 4G **25**
Forest Gdns. PE9: Stam 2B **6**
Forge Cl. PE7: Whit 4D **30**
Forge Ct. PE6: Mkt D 2B **8**
Forge End PE7: Alw 3E **23**

A-Z Peterborough 37

Forli Strada PE7: Hadd 6A 24
Forrest Dr. PE7: Pet 2H 25
Fortuna Dr. PE2: Pet 3D 26
Forty Acre Rd. PE1: Pet 3D 20
Foster Rd. PE2: Pet 5F 19
Foundry Ct. *PE9: Stam* 4E 7
(off Foundry Rd.)
Foundry La. PE9: Stam 4F 7
Foundry Rd. PE9: Stam 4E 7
Fountains Pl. PE6: Eye 1H 15
Four Chimneys Cres. PE7: Pet 5E 25
Fourth Drove PE1: Pet 2F 21
Foxcovert Rd. PE4: Pet 2C 10
PE6: Glin 1C 10
Foxcovert Wlk. PE4: Pet 3D 10
(not continuous)
Fox Dale PE9: Stam 3D 6
Foxdale PE1: Pet 4H 13
Foxglove Cl. PE7: Yax 2G 29
Foxglove Rd. PE9: Stam 2A 6
Foxgloves PE6: Deep J 2E 9
Foxley Cl. PE4: Pet 5E 11
Framlingham Rd. PE2: Pet 2F 27
Francis Gdns. PE1: Pet 3H 13
Franklyn Cres. PE1: Pet 5E 15
Frank Perkins Parkway
PE1: Pet 6F 5 (6B 20)
(not continuous)
PE2: Pet 6B 20
Frank Perkins Way PE1: Pet 2D 20
Fraserburgh Way PE2: Pet 3G 23
Fraser Cl. PE6: Deep J 3E 9
Frederick Dr. PE4: Pet 3E 13
Freesia Way PE7: Yax 3F 29
Freshwater Rd. PE7: Pet 6D 24
Freston PE4: Pet 1H 13
Friary Ct. PE1: Pet 2H 5 (2C 20)
FROGNALL 3H 9
Frognall PE6: Deep J 3H 9
Fryers Callis *PE9: Stam* 5G 7
(off Wothorpe Rd.)
Fulbridge Rd. PE1: Pet 3H 13
PE4: Pet 4E 11
Fulham Rd. PE3: Pet 1G 19
Furze Ride PE1: Pet 3B 14

G

Gainsborough Rd. PE9: Stam 2D 6
Gala Bingo
Peterborough 1G 19
Gale Gdns. PE7: Whit 3C 30
Gallions Cl. PE4: Pet 2F 13
Gannocks, The PE2: Pet 2B 24
Gannocks Cl. PE2: Pet 2B 24
Garden Cl. PE6: Eye 4B 6
Garden Gro. PE7: Whit 4C 30
Garratt Rd. PE9: Stam 5F 7
Garrick Wlk. PE2: Pet 6B 20
Garton End Rd. PE1: Pet 5A 14
Garton St. PE1: Pet 6A 14
Gascoigne PE4: Pet 4B 10
Gas La. PE9: Stam 4G 7
Gas St. PE9: Stam 4G 7
Gatenby Pl. PE4: Pet 5E 11
Gavel St. PE7: Pet 1C 28
Gayton Ct. PE3: Pet 6E 13
Gazeley Gdns. PE7: Far 5C 26
Geddington Rd. PE2: Pet 5G 19
Geneva St. PE1: Pet 2C 4 (2A 20)
George Alcock Way PE7: Far 5D 26
George Gdns. PE7: Whit 2C 30
George Matthews Gdns. PE6: Eye . . .1G 15
George St. PE2: Pet 6B 4 (5H 19)
Georgian Ct. PE3: Pet 4G 19
Giddings Cl. PE2: Pet 3B 24
Giddon's Drove PE6: N'boro 6H 9
Gilbert Cl. PE7: Whit 3C 30
Gildale PE4: Pet 5F 11
Gildenburgh Av. PE1: Pet 6D 14

Gillwell M. PE1: Pet 4G 13
Gilmorton Dr. PE1: Pet 4D 14
Gilpin St. PE1: Pet 5G 13
Gipsy La. PE9: Stam 2H 7
Girton Way PE9: Stam 2E 7
Gladstone St. PE1: Pet 1A 4 (6G 13)
Glamis Gdns. PE3: Pet 3D 18
Glastonbury Cl. PE6: Eye 1G 15
Glatton Dr. PE2: Pet 1D 26
Glebe Av. PE2: Pet 3A 24
Glebe Ct. PE2: Pet 5B 20
Glebe Rd. PE2: Pet 5A 20
Glebe Vw. PE6: Mkt D 2C 8
Glemsford Ri. PE2: Pet 6E 19
Glen, The PE2: Pet 6B 20
Glencoe Way PE2: Pet 4H 23
Glen Cres. PE9: Stam 2G 7
Glendale PE2: Pet 1H 23
Gleneagles PE2: Pet 1B 24
Gleneagles Cl. PE9: Stam 3C 6
Glenfields PE7: Whit 2B 30
Glenton St. PE1: Pet 3G 5 (3C 20)
GLINTON 1B 10
Glinton By-Pass PE4: Milk N, Pea . . .2A 10
PE6: Glin 2A 10
Glinton Rd. PE6: Milk N 1G 11
Global Cen. Ind. Est. PE1: Pet 1E 21
GLOUCESTER CENTRE 1E 25
Gloucester Pl. PE1: Pet 1E 5
Gloucester Rd. PE2: Pet 6B 20
PE9: Stam 3F 7
Glover Dr. PE4: Pet 1B 14
Godric Sq. PE2: Pet 1F 25
Godsey Cres. PE6: Mkt D 3D 8
Godsey La. PE6: Mkt D 2C 8
Godwit Cl. PE7: Whit 1F 31
Goffsmill PE3: Pet 1C 18
Goldcrest Ct. PE1: Pet 3C 14
Goldhay Way PE2: Pet 4A 24
Goldie La. PE2: Pet 1B 24
Goldsmiths La. PE9: Stam 4G 7
Gooches Ct. *PE9: Stam* 5F 7
(off Bath Row)
Goodacre PE2: Pet 3C 24
Goodmans Bus. Pk. PE1: Pet 3E 21
Goodwin Wlk. PE4: Pet 4D 10
Goodwood Rd. PE3: Pet 2B 18
Gordon Av. PE2: Pet 6G 19
Gordon Way PE2: Pet 6E 19
Gorse Grn. PE1: Pet 3B 14
(not continuous)
Gosling Drove PE7: Far 6G 27
Gostwick PE2: Pet 2H 23
Gracechurch Ct. PE1: Pet 6C 14
Gracious St. PE7: Whit 3C 30
Grafham Cl. PE2: Pet 2E 27
Grafton Av. PE3: Pet 2F 19
Granary Cl. PE3: Pet 2A 4 (2G 19)
Granby St. PE1: Pet 4E 5 (3B 20)
Grange Av. PE1: Pet 5A 14
Grange Cres. PE2: Pet 2C 24
Grange Rd. PE3: Pet 2F 19
Gransley Ri. PE2: Pet 6E 13
Granville Av. PE6: N'boro 6F 9
Granville St. PE1: Pet 1D 4 (1A 20)
Grasmere Gdns. PE4: Pet 5F 11
Gravel Wlk. PE1: Pet 5D 4 (4A 20)
Gray Ct. PE1: Pet 4G 13
GREAT CASTERTON 1A 6
Great Casterton Roman Town (remains)
. . . . .1A 6
Great Drove PE7: Yax 4G 29
Gt. Northern Cotts. PE1: Pet 5G 13
Great Nth. Rd. PE7: Ches 2D 22
PE8: Ches, W New 6A 16
PE9: Gt Cas, Stam, Tick 1A 6
Grebe Cl. PE7: Whit 2F 31
Green, The PE4: Pet 6E 11
PE5: Cas 3C 16
PE6: Glin 1A 10
PE7: Yax 4E 29

Greenacres PE4: Pet 5C 10
Green Backyard, The PE2: Pet 5A 20
Green Farm Cl. PE5: Cas 3C 16
Greengate Cl. PE1: Pet 1C 20
Greenham PE3: Pet 2C 18
Green La. PE1: Pet 1A 20
PE7: Yax 3D 28
PE9: Stam 2F 7
Green Man La. PE6: Mar 2A 12
Green Wlk. PE6: Mkt D 3B 8
Greenwood Rd. PE7: Pet 6D 24
Gresham Sq. PE1: Pet 2E 21
Gresley Dr. PE9: Stam 5F 7
Gresley Way PE3: Pet 4E 13
Gretton Cl. PE2: Pet 6E 19
Griffiths Ct. PE2: Pet 2A 24
Grimeshaw Wood Local Nature Reserve
. . . . .4B 12
Grimshaw Rd. PE1: Pet 5B 14
Grimsthorpe Cl. PE6: Mkt D 3B 8
Grove, The PE6: Mkt D 3C 8
PE7: Whit 4E 31
Grove Ct. PE2: Pet 5H 19
Grovelands PE3: Pet 4A 4 (3G 19)
Grove La. PE3: Pet 3C 18
Grove St. PE2: Pet 5H 19
Guelder Rd. PE7: Pet 4F 25
Guildenburgh Cres. PE7: Whit 3E 31
Guildhall Wlk. PE1: Pet 4C 4
Gull Way PE7: Whit 2E 31
Gullymore PE3: Pet 3B 12
GUNTHORPE 1G 13
Gunthorpe Ridings PE4: Pet 6H 11
Gunthorpe Rd. PE4: Pet 1F 13
PE6: Newb 6H 11
Gurnard Leys PE3: Pet 2C 12
Guthlac Av. PE4: Pet 3F 13
Gwash Way PE9: Stam 2H 7

H

Hacke Rd. PE3: Pet 2F 19
Haddonbrook Bus. Cen. PE2: Pet 4G 23
Haddon Cl. PE2: Pet 2E 27
Haddon Rd. PE3: Pet 2G 19
PE9: Stam 3D 6
Haddon Way PE7: Far 5B 26
Hadfield Rd. PE7: Pet 5G 25
Hadley Rd. PE4: Pet 2F 13
Hadrians Ct. PE2: Pet 5B 20
Halesowen Pl. PE6: Eye 1G 15
Half Acre Drove PE7: East 3G 31
Halfleet PE6: Mkt D 2B 8
Halifax Dr. PE6: Mkt D 1D 8
Hallaton Rd. PE1: Pet 3D 14
Hallcroft Rd. PE7: Whit 3B 30
Hall Farm PE6: Mkt D 2C 8
Hallfields La. PE4: Pet 1G 13
Hallidays Yd. *PE9: Stam* 4F 7
(off Radcliffe Rd.)
Hall La. PE4: Pet 5E 11
Hall Meadow Rd. PE6: Deep J 1G 9
Hambleton Rd. PE9: Stam 5C 6
Ham La. PE2: Pet 6H 17
Hammonds Dr. PE1: Pet 6G 5 (4C 20)
HAMPTON 4G 25
HAMPTON CENTRE 5G 25
Hampton Ct. PE3: Pet 5E 13
HAMPTON HARGATE 5E 25
Hampton Leisure Cen. 6F 25
HAMPTON LEYS 5H 25
HAMPTON VALE 6D 24
Hanbury PE2: Pet 4B 24
Hankey St. PE1: Pet 1H 19
Hannington Cl. PE7: Whit 3F 31
Hanover Ct. PE3: Pet 3C 12
PE9: Stam 4G 7
Hansel Cl. PE2: Pet 5G 19
Harcourt Ter. PE9: Stam 4E 7
Hardwick Ct. PE3: Pet 3D 18

Hardwick Rd. PE9: Stam 3D 6
Hardys La. PE7: Whit 4D 30
Harebell Cl. PE1: Pet 2B 14
Harebell Dr. PE7: Yax 2G 29
Harewood Gdns. PE3: Pet 3D 18
Hargate Way PE7: Pet 5D 24
Harlech Grange PE3: Pet 4D 18
Harlton Cl. PE2: Pet 2E 27
Harn Rd. PE7: Pet 5G 25
Harper Cres. PE4: Pet 1B 14
Harpers Cl. PE7: Whit 3C 30
Harrier Pk. PE2: Pet 5H 23
Harrison Cl. PE3: Pet 2B 18
Harris St. PE1: Pet 6H 13
Hartford Ct. PE2: Pet 1D 26
Hartley Av. PE1: Pet 5G 5 (4C 20)
Hart's La. PE7: Whit 3C 30
Hartwell Ct. PE3: Pet 6F 13
Hartwell Way PE3: Pet 5D 12
Harvester Pl. PE1: Pet 1E 19
Harvester Rd. PE7: Whit 2B 30
Harvester Way PE1: Pet 4G 5 (4C 20)
Hastings Rd. PE4: Pet 1E 13
Havelock Dr. PE2: Pet 1E 27
Haveswater Cl. PE4: Pet 1G 13
Hawksbill Way PE7: Pet 6D 4 (5A 20)
Hawkshead Way PE4: Pet 6G 11
Hawthorn Cl. PE6: Mkt D 2C 8
Hawthorn Dr. PE7: Whit 4E 31
Hawthornes, The PE6: Mkt D 2B 8
Hawthorn Rd. PE1: Pet 5C 14
   PE7: Yax .4F 29
Hayward PE3: Pet 1E 19
Haywardsfield PE3: Pet 4C 18
Hazel Cft. PE9: Stam 4F 7
   (off Radcliffe Rd.)
Hazel Cft. PE4: Pet 5C 10
Hazel Gro. PE9: Stam 3B 6
Headlands Way PE7: Whit 2C 30
Heather Av. PE1: Pet 3A 14
Heatherdale Cl. PE7: Far 2C 26
Heath Row PE1: Pet 2B 14
Heaton Cl. PE3: Pet 2D 18
Hedda Dr. PE7: Pet 4F 25
Hedgelands PE4: Pet 4E 11
Helmsdale Gdns. PE4: Pet 1D 12
Helmsley Ct. PE2: Pet 1F 27
Helpston Rd. PE5: Ail, Mar 3B 16
   PE6: Ail, Mar 3B 16
   PE6: Glin 1A 10
   (not continuous)
Heltwate PE3: Pet 4D 12
Hemingford Cres. PE2: Pet 1E 27
Hemmerley Dr. PE7: Whit 2D 30
Hempsted Rd. PE7: Pet 6E 25
Henry Ct. PE1: Pet 1C 4 (1A 20)
Henry Penn Wlk. PE1: Pet 6C 4
Henry St. PE1: Pet 1A 20
Henshaw PE1: Pet 5E 15
Henson Dr. PE7: Pet 1A 26
Herald Way PE4: Pet 6H 11
Hercules Way PE2: Pet 4E 27
Hereward Arc. PE1: Pet 3D 4
Hereward Cl. PE1: Pet 4F 5 (3B 20)
Hereward Cross PE1: Pet 3D 4 (3A 20)
Hereward Rd. PE1: Pet 4F 5 (3B 20)
Hereward Way PE6: Deep J 4F 9
Heritage Ct. PE1: Pet 6C 14
Herlington Pl. PE2: Pet 3D 24
Herlington Cen. PE2: Pet 3D 24
Hermitage, The PE9: Stam 4D 6
Heron Cl. PE7: Whit 2E 31
Heron Ct. PE2: Pet 1D 26
Heron Pk. PE1: Pet 5F 15
Heronry Dr. PE6: Mar 3A 18
Herrick Cl. PE1: Pet 3G 13
Hetley PE2: Pet 5E 15
Hexham Ct. PE1: Pet 1H 5 (2D 20)
Heyford Cl. PE4: Pet 1H 13
Hickling Wlk. PE4: Pet 6G 11
Hicks La. PE7: Pet 2H 25

Highbury St. PE1: Pet 6H 13
High Causeway PE7: Whit 3D 30
   (not continuous)
Highclere Rd. PE7: Pet 4F 25
High Ct. Way PE7: Pet 1D 28
Highfield Wlk. PE7: Yax 3G 29
Highgrove Gdns. PE9: Stam 4C 6
High St. PE2: Pet 1H 25
   PE5: Cas 3D 16
   PE6: Eye .1G 15
   PE6: Glin 1A 10
   PE6: Mkt D, Deep J 4D 8
   PE9: Stam 4F 7
High St. St Martin's PE9: Stam 5G 7
Higney Rd. PE7: Pet 6E 25
Hillary Cl. PE7: Pet 2A 26
   PE9: Stam 3H 7
Hill Cl. PE1: Pet 6D 14
Hillcrest Av. PE7: Yax 4E 29
Hillside Wlk. PE7: Yax 3G 29
Hills Yd. PE1: Pet 5C 4
Hillward Cl. PE2: Pet 1E 25
Hinchcliffe PE2: Pet 4A 24
Hinton Cl. PE7: Whit 2C 30
HMP Peterborough PE3: Pet 6F 13
Hod Fen Drove PE7: Yax 6E 29
Hodgson Av. PE4: Pet 3C 10
Hodgson Cen. PE4: Pet 3D 10
Hodney Rd. PE6: Eye 1F 15
   (not continuous)
Hog Fen Drove PE7: Yax 4G 29
Holcroft PE2: Pet 4D 24
Holdfield PE3: Pet 5D 12
Holdich St. PE3: Pet 3A 4 (3G 19)
Holgate La. PE4: Pet 2D 10
Holkham Rd. PE2: Pet 4H 23
Holland Av. PE4: Pet 2F 13
Holland Cl. PE4: Pet 2F 13
   PE6: Mkt D 2B 8
   PE7: Whit 2B 30
Holland Rd. PE9: Stam 3G 7
Hollowside Rd. PE7: Pet 1B 28
Holly Wlk. PE7: Pet 4F 25
Holly Way PE6: Deep J 4E 9
Holme Cl. PE5: Ail 3B 16
   PE9: Tin 6B 6
Holme Rd. PE7: Yax 5E 29
Holmes Rd. PE6: Glin 2B 10
Holmes Way PE4: Pet 1G 13
Holywell Cl. PE3: Pet 4C 18
Holywell Way PE3: Pet 3B 18
Home Farm Cl. PE9: Gt Cas 1A 6
Home Pasture PE4: Pet 4D 10
Honeyhill PE4: Pet 2A 14
Honeysuckle Ct. PE2: Pet 6G 19
Hornbeam Rd. PE7: Pet 5E 25
Horsegate PE6: Deep J 4E 9
   PE7: Whit 3C 30
Horsegate Farm Cl. PE6: Deep J 4E 9
Horsegate La. PE7: Whit 3C 30
Horseshoe La. PE9: Stam 4F 7
   (off Sheep Mkt.)
Horseshoe Way PE7: Pet 6F 25
Horton Wlk. PE3: Pet 6F 13
Houghton Av. PE2: Pet 2F 27
Howegate Dr. PE7: Pet 6D 24
Howland PE2: Pet 4C 24
Hoylake Dr. PE7: Far 2C 26
Hubberts Ct. PE1: Pet 1F 5
Hudson Gro. PE7: Pet 3H 25
Humber Dr. PE7: Yax 3E 29
Humphrys St. PE2: Pet 5F 19
Hungarton Ct. PE1: Pet 3D 14
Hunsbury Cl. PE7: Whit 5E 31
Hunting Av. PE2: Pet 6H 19
Huntly Gro. PE1: Pet 1A 20
Huntly Rd. PE2: Pet 6G 19
Huntly Sq. PE2: Pet 3A 24
   (off Cherry Orton Rd.)
Huntsmans Ga. PE3: Pet 2A 18

Hurn Rd. PE6: Mar, Pet 1A 12
Hyholmes PE3: Pet 4B 12
Hythegate PE4: Pet 5F 11

I

Ibbott Cl. PE2: Pet 2E 27
Ihlee Cl. PE4: Pet 2G 13
Ilex Cl. PE7: Pet 4E 25
Iliffe Ga. PE4: Pet 1H 13
Illston Pl. PE1: Pet 4E 15
Imperial Way PE7: Yax 2H 29
Ingleborough PE1: Pet 6A 14
Inhams Cl. PE7: Whit 4D 30
INHAM'S END 4E 31
Inham's Rd. PE7: Whit 4D 30
Innovation Way PE2: Pet 2F 23
Irchester Pl. PE3: Pet 6F 13
Ireland Ho. PE1: Pet 4E 5
Irnham Rd. PE9: Stam 2G 7
Ironmonger St. PE9: Stam 4G 7
Irving Burgess Cl. PE7: Whit 2B 30
Isham Rd. PE3: Pet 1F 19
Isherwood Cl. PE1: Pet 5A 14
Isis Way PE2: Alw 2F 23
Itter Cres. PE4: Pet 2G 13
Ivatt Way PE3: Pet 4F 13
Ivatt Way Ind. Cen. PE3: Pet 5F 13
Ivy Gro. PE4: Pet 1F 13
Ivy La. PE7: Whit 3C 30
Ixworth Cl. PE6: Eye 1G 15

J

Jack Hunt Pool & Gym 2D 18
Jackson Way PE9: Stam 3D 6
James Av. PE1: Pet 5G 5 (4C 20)
James Gdns. PE7: Whit 3D 30
Jasmine Ct. PE2: Pet 5A 24
Jasmine Way PE7: Yax 2F 29
Jellings Pl. PE1: Pet 1A 20
Joan Wake Cl. PE6: Mkt D 2C 8
John Bird Wlk. PE7: Far 5C 26
John Eve Way PE6: Mkt D 2C 8
John King Gdns. PE2: Pet 1C 26
Johnson Wlk. PE1: Pet 4H 13
John Wesley Rd. PE4: Pet 6C 10
Jones Hill PE7: Pet 1A 28
Jones La. PE7: East 3H 31
Jordan M. PE1: Pet 2E 5 (2B 20)
Jorose Way PE3: Pet 2C 18
Joseph Odam Way PE2: Pet 3F 23
Jubilee Ct. PE3: Pet 4D 12
Jubilee Dr. PE6: Mkt D 2D 8
Jubilee Mans. PE3: Pet 3F 19
Jubilee St. PE2: Pet 6A 4 (5H 19)
Juniper Cres. PE3: Pet 3C 18
Juno Way PE2: Pet 3D 26
Jupiter Av. PE2: Pet 3C 26
Jury Rd. PE7: Pet 1C 28
Justice Way PE7: Pet 1B 28

K

Kariba Ct. PE2: Pet 5H 19
Katharine Way PE3: Pet 6C 12
Katia Pl. PE2: Pet 3C 26
Keats Gro. PE9: Stam 4C 6
Keats Way PE1: Pet 4G 13
Keble Cl. PE9: Stam 2E 7
Keble Ct. PE9: Stam 2E 7
Kedleston Rd. PE2: Pet 1F 27
Keeton Rd. PE1: Pet 4G 13
Kelburn Rd. PE2: Pet 2G 23
Kelful Cl. PE7: East 3H 31
Kelso Ct. PE4: Pet 2E 13
Kendal Cl. PE4: Pet 1H 13

Kendall Cft. PE7: Whit 4D **30**
Kendrick Cl. PE2: Pet 1D **26**
Kenilworth Av. PE2: Pet 2G **27**
Kennedy St. PE7: Pet 6D **24**
Kennels Dr. PE6: Mar 1H **17**
Kennet Gdns. PE4: Pet 2G **13**
Kentmere Pl. PE4: Pet 1H **13**
Kent Rd. PE3: Pet 3A **4** (3G **19**)
Kesteven Cl. PE6: Deep J 3D **8**
Kesteven Dr. PE6: Mkt D 2B **8**
Kesteven Rd. PE9: Stam 2F **7**
Kesteven Wlk. PE1: Pet 3E **5** (3B **20**)
Kestrel Ct. PE3: Pet 3C **18**
Kestrel Rd. PE7: Yax 1H **29**
Keswick Cl. PE4: Pet 6H **11**
Kettering Rd. PE9: Wot, Stam 6F **7**
Keyham PE1: Pet 3G **5**
Keys Pk. PE1: Pet 4F **15**
Key Theatre 6D **4** (4B **20**)
Kilbride Way PE2: Pet 3G **23**
Kildare Dr. PE3: Pet 1E **19**
Kilham PE2: Pet 5A **24**
Kiln St. PE7: Pet 6D **24**
Kilverstone PE4: Pet 2D **10**
Kimbolton Ct. PE1: Pet 1B **4** (2H **19**)
Kingfisher Cl. PE7: Yax 3D **28**
Kingfisher Ct. *PE2: Pet* *6D **20***
(off Thistle Dr.)
Kingfisher Rd. PE7: Whit 2E **31**
Kingfishers PE2: Pet 1H **23**
King Henry Chase PE3: Pet 6C **12**
Kings Acre PE5: Ail 3B **16**
Kingsbridge Cen., The PE3: Pet . . .3E **13**
Kingsbridge Ct. PE4: Pet 4C **10**
King's Delph PE7: Whit 2H **27**
King's Delph Drove PE7: Far 6E **27**
King's Delph Highway PE7: Far 5G **27**
Kings Dyke Cl. PE2: Pet 1E **27**
King's Gdns. PE1: Pet 6A **14**
Kingsgate PE6: Mkt D 2C **8**
Kingsley Rd. PE1: Pet 1G **5** (1C **20**)
Kings Mill La. PE9: Stam 5F **7**
Kings Rd. PE2: Pet 1B **26**
PE9: Stam 3F **7**
Kingston Dr. PE2: Pet 2E **27**
KINGSTON PARK 3B **26**
King St. PE1: Pet 4C **4** (3H **19**)
Kinnears Wlk. PE2: Pet 5B **24**
Kipling Cl. PE9: Stam 1H **7**
Kipling Ct. PE1: Pet 3G **13**
Kirby Wlk. PE3: Pet 1E **19**
Kirkmeadow PE3: Pet 3C **12**
Kirkstall PE2: Pet 4D **24**
Kirkton Ga. PE3: Pet 4C **18**
Kirkwood Cl. PE3: Pet 4A **4** (4G **19**)
Knight Cl. PE6: Deep J 3E **9**
Knighton Cl. PE7: Pet 6F **25**
Knights M. PE2: Pet 1A **26**
Knole Wlk. PE3: Pet 2D **18**

Lambeth Wlk. PE9: Stam 3E **7**
Lammas Rd. PE1: Pet 4A **14**
Lamport Cl. PE6: Mkt D 2B **8**
Lancashire Ga. PE1: Pet 4F **5** (3B **20**)
Lancaster Ct. PE7: Yax 3G **29**
Lancaster Rd. PE9: Stam 3F **7**
Lancaster Wlk. PE7: Yax 3F **29**
Lancaster Way PE6: Mkt D 1C **8**
PE7: Yax 3F **29**
Lancing Cl. PE4: Pet 6E **11**
Lander Cres. PE7: Yax 2A **26**
Landsdowne Rd. PE7: Yax 3F **29**
Landy Grn. Way PE5: Cas 5E **17**
Langdyke PE1: Pet 5F **15**
Langford Rd. PE2: Pet 6A **20**
Langley PE3: Pet 3D **12**
(not continuous)
Langton Rd. PE1: Pet 4D **14**
Lansdowne Wlk. PE2: Pet 6F **19**
Lapwing Dr. PE7: Whit 1F **31**
Larch Cl. PE7: Yax 3F **29**
Larch Gro. PE1: Pet 5C **14**
Lares Av. PE2: Pet 3D **26**
Larklands PE3: Pet 4D **18**
Lark Ri. PE6: Mkt D 3D **8**
Larkspur Wlk. PE4: Pet 6F **11**
Latham Av. PE2: Pet 1E **25**
Lattersey Cl. PE7: Whit 3E **31**
LATTERSEY FIELD 4F **31**
Lattersey Hill Trad. Est. PE7: Whit . .6F **31**
Lattersey Nature Reserve 5F **31**
Laughton Dr. PE9: Stam 3C **6**
Launde Gdns. PE9: Stam 5C **6**
Laurel Cl. PE7: Yax 5D **28**
Lavender Cl. PE7: Yax 3F **29**
Lavender Cres. PE1: Pet 3A **14**
Lavender Way PE9: Stam 2B **6**
Lavenham Ct. PE2: Pet 6E **19**
Lavington Grange PE1: Pet 5E **15**
Lawn Av. PE1: Pet 4A **14**
Lawn Cl. PE7: Yax 5E **29**
Lawns, The PE4: Pet 2G **13**
Lawrence Av. PE7: Far 5C **26**
Law's Cl. PE6: Milk N 1H **11**
Lawson Av. PE7: Pet 1D **26**
Laxton Cl. PE6: Deep J 3G **9**
Laxton Sq. PE1: Pet 3D **4** (3A **20**)
Leading Drove PE7: Yax 6D **28**
(not continuous)
Leaf Av. PE7: Pet 4F **25**
Lea Gdns. PE3: Pet 5A **4** (4H **19**)
Ledbury Rd. PE3: Pet 2D **18**
Ledham PE2: Pet 3H **23**
Leeder Cl. PE7: Far 6D **26**
Lee Rd. PE7: Yax 5E **29**
Lees, The PE6: Deep J 3F **9**
Leeson Ho. PE1: Pet 3E **5**
Leeward Gdns. PE7: Whit 4D **30**
Leicester Ter. PE1: Pet 1E **5**
Leighton PE2: Pet 3E **25**
Leinsters Cl. PE3: Pet 3F **19**
Leiston Ct. PE6: Eye 2G **15**
Leofric Sq. PE1: Pet 2E **21**
Leon Dr. PE2: Pet 3C **26**
Lessingham PE2: Pet 3H **23**
Lethbridge Rd. PE4: Pet 1G **13**
Levens Wlk. PE3: Pet 2D **18**
Lewes Gdns. PE4: Pet 6E **11**
Leys, The PE3: Pet 4C **18**
Libertas Dr. PE3: Pet 3E **27**
Lichfield Av. PE4: Pet 6D **10**
Lidgate Cl. PE2: Pet 5E **19**
Lido, The 5E **5** (4B **20**)
Lilac Rd. PE1: Pet 4C **14**
Lilac Wlk. PE7: Yax 3F **29**
Lima Way PE2: Pet 3D **26**
Lime Kiln Cl. PE3: Pet 1G **19**
Limes, The PE5: Cas 4D **16**
PE7: Whit 5C **30**
Limesquare Bus. Pk. PE3: Pet 6F **13**

Lime Tree Av. PE1: Pet 1H **19**
PE6: Mkt D 2B **8**
Lime Tree Cl. PE7: Yax 2F **29**
Linchfield Cl. PE6: Deep J 3F **9**
Linchfield Rd. PE6: Deep J 1E **9**
Lincoln Cl. PE6: Mkt D 2B **8**
Lincoln Ct. PE1: Pet 2C **4**
Lincoln Ga. PE1: Pet 1C **4** (2A **20**)
Lincoln Rd. PE1: Pet 3C **4** (4F **13**)
PE4: Pet 5C **10**
(not continuous)
PE6: Deep G, Glin, N'boro 4C **8**
(not continuous)
PE6: Glin, Pet 1A **10**
(not continuous)
PE9: Stam 2G **7**
Linden Gdns. PE2: Pet 2G **23**
Lindens, The PE1: Pet 1C **4** (2A **20**)
Lindisfarne Rd. PE6: Eye 2G **15**
Lindridge Wlk. PE3: Pet 2C **18**
Lindsey Av. PE6: Mkt D 2B **8**
Lindsey Cl. PE4: Pet 2F **13**
Lindsey Ct. PE6: Deep J 4F **9**
Lindsey Rd. PE9: Stam 3G **7**
Ling Gth. PE1: Pet 3B **14**
Lingwood Pk. PE3: Pet 5C **18**
Link Rd. PE1: Pet 1A **4** (2H **19**)
Linkside PE3: Pet 2D **12**
Linley Rd. PE7: Whit 4D **30**
Linnet PE2: Pet 1H **23**
Linnet Cl. PE6: Deep J 3D **8**
Lister Rd. PE1: Pet 4H **13**
Litchfield Cl. PE7: Yax 4F **29**
Lit. Casterton Rd. PE9: Lit C 1D **6**
Little Cl. PE6: Eye 2H **15**
Littlecote Gro. PE4: Pet 3G **13**
Littledale Cres. PE2: Pet 1H **25**
Lit. Johns Cl. PE3: Pet 2B **18**
Littlemeer PE2: Pet 3B **24**
Livermore Grn. PE4: Pet 3C **10**
Livingstone Rd. PE7: Yax 4D **28**
Loch Fyne Cl. PE2: Pet 3F **23**
Loch Lomond Way PE2: Pet 3F **23**
Locks Cl. PE6: Deep J 5H **9**
Lode Cl. PE7: Far 3C **26**
Loder Av. PE3: Pet 3B **18**
Loire Ct. PE1: Pet 1G **19**
Lombardy Dr. PE1: Pet 3C **14**
London Rd. PE2: Pet 6D **4** (3H **25**)
PE7: Nor X, Pet, Yax 6A **28**
PE7: Pet, Yax 2D **28**
PE9: Stam 6G **7**
London St. PE7: Whit 4C **30**
Long Causeway PE1: Pet 4C **4** (3A **20**)
Long Drove PE7: Whit 1D **30**
Longfield Ga. PE2: Pet 2C **24**
Long Pasture PE4: Pet 4D **10**
LONGTHORPE 4C **18**
Longthorpe Cl. PE3: Pet 3C **18**
Longthorpe Grn. PE3: Pet 4D **18**
Longthorpe Ho. PE3: Pet 3B **18**
Longthorpe Ho. M. PE3: Pet 3B **18**
Longthorpe Parkway PE3: Pet 5D **18**
Longthorpe Tower 4C **18**
Longueville Ct. PE2: Pet 2E **25**
Longwater PE2: Pet 1D **24**
Lonsdale Rd. PE9: Stam 4C **6**
Lord Burghley's Hospital *PE9: Stam* . .*5G **7***
(off Station Rd.)
Lornas Fld. PE7: Pet 4F **25**
Losecoat Cl. PE9: Stam 1H **7**
Love La. PE7: Whit 4C **30**
Lovells Ct. *PE7: Whit* *3D **30***
(off High Causeway)
Low Cross PE7: Whit 2C **30**
Lowick Gdns. PE3: Pet 6E **13**
Lowther Gdns. PE4: Pet 1F **13**
Loxley PE4: Pet 5C **10**
Lucina Dr. PE2: Pet 3D **26**
Luddington Rd. PE4: Pet 2F **13**
Ludlow M. PE3: Pet 4A **4** (3H **19**)

L

Laburnum Av. PE7: Yax 3F **29**
Laburnum Gro. PE1: Pet 3B **14**
Laburnum Wlk. PE9: Stam 3F **7**
Ladybower Way PE4: Pet 6G **11**
Lady Charlotte Rd. PE7: Pet 4E **25**
Lady Lodge Dr. PE2: Pet 2C **24**
Lady Margaret's Av.
PE6: Mkt D, Deep J 3D **8**
Lady Romayne Cl. PE9: Stam 5G **7**
Ladysmith Av. PE7: Whit 2E **31**
Lakefield Rd. PE7: Pet 1B **28**
Lakeside PE4: Pet 5F **11**
Lakeside Superbowl
Peterborough 3E **5**
Lakeview Way PE7: Pet 5E **25**
(not continuous)
Lambert M. PE9: Stam 5G **7**
Lambes Ct. PE4: Pet 5C **10**

Luffenham Cl. PE9: Stam	4C **6**
Lumby's Ter. *PE9: Stam*	5G **7**
	(off Water St.)
Luna Way PE2: Pet	3D **26**
Lutton Gro. PE3: Pet	6E **13**
Lyme Wlk. PE3: Pet	1E **19**
Lynch Cotts. PE2: Pet	1G **23**
LYNCH WOOD	2G **23**
Lynch Wood PE2: Pet	2F **23**
Lyndale Pk. PE2: Pet	1G **23**
Lyndon Way PE9: Stam	4C **6**
Lynton Rd. PE1: Pet	5H **13**
Lysander Dr. PE6: Mkt D	1D **8**
Lythemere PE2: Pet	3E **25**
Lyvelly Gdns. PE1: Pet	5E **15**

M

Mace Rd. PE2: Pet	2D **26**
McIntyre Ct. PE1: Pet	6C **14**
Maffit Rd. PE5: Ail	2B **16**
Magdellan Ct. PE3: Pet	3G **19**
Magee Rd. PE4: Pet	2F **13**
Magistrates' Court	
Peterborough	5D **4** (4A **20**)
Stamford	4G **7**
	(off St Mary's Hill)
Magistrates Rd. PE7: Pet	1D **28**
Magnolia Av. PE3: Pet	3C **18**
Magnus Cl. PE2: Pet	3C **26**
Maiden La. PE9: Stam	4G **7**
Main St. PE5: Ail	3B **16**
PE7: Far	5C **26**
PE7: Yax	5E **29**
PE9: Gt Cas	1A **6**
PE9: Tin	6A **6**
Malborne Way PE2: Pet	4D **24**
Mallard Bus. Cen.	
PE3: Pet	2C **12**
Mallard Cl. PE7: Whit	2E **31**
Mallard Ct. PE9: Stam	5F **7**
Mallard Rd. PE3: Pet	2C **12**
Mallory Dr. PE7: Yax	4D **28**
Mallory La. *PE9: Stam*	4F **7**
	(off All Saints St.)
Mallory Rd. PE1: Pet	3H **5** (3D **20**)
Malmesbury Dr. PE6: Eye	1H **15**
Maltings, The *PE9: Stam*	5G **7**
	(off Water St.)
PE9: Wot	6G **7**
Malting Sq. PE7: Yax	3F **29**
Maltings Yd. PE9: Stam	5G **7**
Malus Cl. PE2: Pet	4E **25**
Malvern Rd. PE4: Pet	1G **13**
Manasty Rd. PE2: Pet	5G **23**
Mancetter Sq. PE4: Pet	2D **12**
Mandeville PE2: Pet	3B **24**
Manku Cl. PE1: Pet	1F **5**
Manor Av. PE2: Pet	6B **20**
Manor Cl. PE7: Far	5C **26**
PE7: Yax	4D **28**
Manor Dr. PE4: Pet	6H **11** & 1A **14**
Mnr. Farm La. PE5: Cas	3C **16**
Manor Gdns. PE2: Pet	6C **20**
Manor Gro. Cen., The	
PE1: Pet	2E **21**
Manor Ho. Cl. PE6: Deep J	4F **9**
Manor Ho. St. PE1: Pet	2C **4** (2A **20**)
Manor Leisure Cen.	4D **30**
Manor Vw. PE7: Whit	4C **30**
Manor Way PE6: Deep J	4F **9**
Mansfield Ct. PE1: Pet	6C **14**
Manton PE3: Pet	2C **18**
Maple Ct. PE7: Yax	3F **29**
Maple Gro. PE1: Pet	4B **14**
Maples, The PE1: Pet	6F **15**
PE2: Pet	3B **24**
Marconi Dr. PE7: Yax	3D **28**
Mardale Gdns. PE4: Pet	1H **13**
Margam Cl. PE6: Eye	1G **15**

Marholm Rd. PE3: Pet	2C **12**
PE4: Pet	2D **12**
PE5: Cas	4F **17**
PE6: Cas	2E **17**
Marigold Cl. PE9: Stam	3A **6**
Marigolds PE6: Deep J	2E **9**
Marius Cres. PE7: Pet	4E **25**
MARKET DEEPING	3C **8**
Market Deeping By-Pass PE6: Max	4B **8**
PE6: Mkt D	1B **8**
Market Ga. PE6: Mkt D	4C **8**
Market Pl. PE6: Mkt D	4C **8**
PE7: Whit	3C **30**
Marketstede PE7: Pet	5D **24**
Market St. PE7: Whit	3C **30**
Markham Retail Pk. PE9: Stam	2H **7**
Marlborough Cl. PE7: Yax	4E **29**
Marlowe Gro. PE4: Pet	3G **13**
Marne Av. PE4: Pet	2E **13**
Marne Rd. PE7: Whit	5E **31**
Marriott Ct. PE1: Pet	6E **15**
Marshall's Way PE7: Far	5C **26**
Marsham PE2: Pet	4B **24**
Martin Ct. PE4: Pet	4B **12**
PE7: Whit	3C **30**
Martin Markham Ind. Est.	
PE9: Stam	2H **7**
Martinsbridge PE1: Pet	4F **15**
Martins Way PE2: Pet	2B **24**
Mary Armyne Rd. PE2: Pet	2D **24**
Mary Walsham Cl. PE2: Pet	2E **27**
Maskew Av. PE1: Pet	4F **13**
Maskew Retail Pk. PE1: Pet	5F **13**
Mason Dr. PE9: Stam	3D **6**
Mason Gro. PE4: Pet	1B **14**
Masterton Cl. PE9: Stam	2H **7**
Masterton Rd. PE9: Stam	2G **7**
Matley PE2: Pet	2A **24**
Maud Swift Ct. PE2: Pet	1B **26**
Maxey Cl. PE6: Mkt D	3B **8**
Maxey Vw. PE6: Deep G	5D **8**
Maxwell Rd. PE2: Pet	1F **25**
Mayfield Rd. PE1: Pet	4A **14**
PE7: East	3H **31**
Mayor's Wlk. PE1: Pet	1A **4** (2F **19**)
PE3: Pet	1A **4** (2F **19**)
Mead, The PE4: Pet	2D **12**
Mead Cl. PE4: Pet	2D **12**
Meadenvale PE1: Pet	5F **15**
Meadow Gro. PE1: Pet	2B **14**
Meadow Rd. PE6: Milk N, Pea	1E **11**
PE6: Mkt D	3D **8**
Meadows, The PE2: Pet	2B **24**
PE6: Mkt D	3D **8**
Meadowsweet PE9: Stam	2A **6**
Meadow Vw. PE7: Whit	2D **30**
PE9: Stam	3H **7**
Meadow Wlk. PE7: Yax	3G **29**
Meadway PE6: Mkt D	2B **8**
Mealsgate PE4: Pet	1H **13**
Medbourne Gdns. PE1: Pet	3D **14**
Medeswell PE2: Pet	3E **25**
	(not continuous)
Medworth PE2: Pet	4B **24**
Meggan Ga. PE3: Pet	4C **18**
Melancholy Wlk. PE9: Stam	5F **7**
Melbourne Rd. PE9: Stam	3H **7**
Melford Cl. PE3: Pet	4C **18**
Mellows Cl. PE1: Pet	2H **5** (2C **20**)
Mellows Ct. PE1: Pet	2H **5** (2C **20**)
Melrose Cl. PE9: Stam	3C **6**
Melrose Dr. PE2: Pet	6A **20**
Mendip Gro. PE4: Pet	1G **13**
Mercian Ct. PE2: Pet	6D **20**
Mercury Cl. PE2: Pet	3C **26**
Mere Drove PE7: Yax	5F **29**
Merefield Vw. PE7: Whit	2D **30**
Merelade Gro. PE4: Pet	4C **10**
Merevale Dr. PE6: Eye	1H **15**

Mere Vw. PE7: Yax	3G **29**
Mere Vw. Ind. Est. PE7: Yax	3G **29**
Meriton PE2: Pet	4B **24**
Metro Cen., The PE2: Pet	1F **25**
Mewburn PE3: Pet	2C **12**
Meynell Wlk. PE3: Pet	2E **19**
	(not continuous)
Michael Taylor Cl. PE3: Pet	3F **19**
Mickle Ga. PE7: Pet	4C **18**
Middlefield PE7: Pet	4F **25**
Middleham Cl. PE2: Pet	2F **27**
Middle Pasture PE4: Pet	4D **10**
Middle Rd. PE6: Newb	1H **11**
Middle St. PE7: Far	5C **26**
Middleton PE3: Pet	1C **18**
Middletons Rd. PE7: Yax	4E **29**
Midgate PE11: Pet	3D **4** (3A **20**)
Midgate Ho. PE1: Pet	3D **4** (3A **20**)
Midland Rd. PE3: Pet	2A **4** (2G **19**)
Mid Water Cres. PE7: Pet	6D **24**
Milby Drove PE7: Far	5F **27**
Mildmay Rd. PE4: Pet	3F **13**
Mile Drove PE7: Yax	4H **29**
Milk and Water Drove PE7: Far	5G **27**
MILKING NOOK	1G **11**
Milking Nook Rd. PE6: Milk N	1G **11**
Mill Cres. PE2: Pet	3A **24**
Miller Way PE1: Pet	5G **5** (4C **20**)
MILLFIELD	6H **13**
Millfield Rd. PE6: Deep J	4F **9**
PE6: Mkt D	2A **8**
Millfield Way PE7: Whit	4E **31**
	(not continuous)
Mill La. PE5: Cas	6D **16**
PE7: Alw	2E **23**
PE8: W New	6A **16**
PE9: Tin	6B **6**
Millport Dr. PE6: Eye	1H **15**
Mill Rd. PE2: Pet	3A **24**
PE6: Max	6A **8**
PE7: Whit	4D **30**
Millview PE7: Alw	2E **23**
Millwood Gdns. PE3: Pet	3C **18**
Milners Ct. *PE9: Stam*	4G **7**
	(off Gas St.)
Milnyard Sq. PE2: Pet	5G **23**
Milton Bus. Pk. PE1: Pet	4E **21**
Milton La. PE5: Cas	4C **16**
Milton Rd. PE2: Pet	6A **20**
Milton Way PE3: Pet	2A **18**
Mina Cl. PE2: Pet	3D **26**
Minerva Bus. Pk. PE2: Alw	2F **23**
Minster Precincts PE1: Pet	4D **4** (3A **20**)
Miral Ct. PE1: Pet	1A **20**
Misterton PE2: Pet	4A **24**
Misterton Ct. PE2: Pet	4A **24**
Mitchell Cl. PE7: Pet	4G **5** (3C **20**)
Moggswell La. PE2: Pet	3D **24**
Molyneux Sq. PE7: Pet	1B **28**
Monarch Av. PE2: Pet	1A **26**
Monks Cl. PE7: Whit	2C **30**
Monks Dr. PE6: Eye	2G **15**
Monksfield M. PE1: Pet	2H **5** (2C **20**)
Monks Gro. PE4: Pet	4C **10**
Monkstone Ho. PE1: Pet	3D **4** (3A **20**)
Montague Ho. PE1: Pet	4E **5**
Montagu Rd. PE4: Pet	3F **13**
Montrose Cl. PE9: Stam	3C **6**
Monument Ct. PE1: Pet	1E **5**
Monument St. PE1: Pet	1D **4** (2A **20**)
	(not continuous)
Moore's La. PE6: Eye	1H **15**
Moorfield Rd. PE3: Pet	2F **19**
Moorhen Rd. PE7: Whit	1E **31**
Moorland Ct. PE4: Pet	5D **10**
Moray Cl. PE9: Stam	3B **6**
Morborne Cl. PE2: Pet	1D **26**
Morborne Rd. PE7: Pet	5E **25**
Moresby Way PE7: Pet	2A **26**
Moreton's Cl. PE7: Whit	2E **31**
Morgan Cl. PE7: Yax	3E **29**

Morley Way PE2: Pet 2F 25
Morpeth Cl. PE2: Pet 1E 25
Morpeth Rd. PE3: Pet 2E 19
Morris Cl. PE7: Whit 2B 30
Morris Ct. PE7: Yax 3E 29
Morris St. PE1: Pet 3F 5 (2B 20)
Mosel Wlk. PE2: Pet 5G 19
Moulton Gro. PE3: Pet 5E 13
Mountbatten Av. PE7: Yax 4E 29
   PE9: Stam 3E 7
Mountbatten Way PE3: Pet 5E 13
   PE7: Whit 4F 31
Mt. Pleasant PE2: Pet 6C 20
Mountsteven Av. PE4: Pet 2E 13
Mountsteven Ho. PE1: Pet 4E 5
Mowbray Rd. PE6: Pet 2B 12
Mulberry Cl. PE7: Whit 5E 31
   PE7: Yax 3G 29
Mulberry Gdns. PE4: Pet 2G 13
Munday Gdns. PE7: Whit 2D 30
Muntjac Cl. PE3: Pet 6C 12
Muskham PE3: Pet 1B 18
Muswell Rd. PE3: Pet 1G 19
Myrtle Av. PE1: Pet 4B 14
Myrtle Ct. PE1: Pet 4C 14
Myrtle Gro. PE1: Pet 4C 14
Myrtle Ho. Cvn. Pk. PE1: Pet 6F 15

N

Nab La. PE4: Pet 2H 13
Nags Head Pas. PE9: Stam 4G 7
   (off Ironmonger St.)
Nairn Dr. PE2: Pet 3H 23
Nairn Rd. PE9: Stam 4C 6
Nansicles Rd. PE2: Pet 1F 25
Napier Pl. PE2: Pet 1G 23
Narrow Drove PE7: Yax 4H 29
Naseby Cl. PE3: Pet 6E 13
Nathan Cl. PE3: Pet 3C 18
Natures Way PE7: Pet 5D 24
Neath Ct. PE6: Eye 1H 15
Neaverson Rd. PE6: Glin 2B 10
Needham Ct. PE7: Yax 5E 29
Nelson Pl. PE2: Pet 1E 27
Nene Cl. PE7: Whit 4D 30
Nene Ct. PE9: Stam 4E 7
Nene Parkway PE2: Pet 1D 24
   PE3: Pet 4B 18
Nene St. PE1: Pet 3G 5 (3C 20)
Nene Valley Railway
   Ferry Meadows Station 6A 18
   Orton Mere Station 6D 18
   Peterborough (Nene Valley) Station
   . . . . .6B 4 (4H 19)
Neptune Cl. PE2: Pet 3D 26
NETHERTON 2G 19
NEWARK .6D 14
Newark Av. PE1: Pet 5B 14
Newark Cen., The PE1: Pet 6F 15
Newark Rd. PE1: Pet 6E 15
Newborn Cl. PE2: Pet 2E 27
NEWBOROUGH FEN 3H 11
Newborough Rd. PE4: Pet 1C 14
Newboults La. PE9: Stam 4E 7
Newby Cl. PE3: Pet 2D 18
Newcastle Dr. PE2: Pet 1F 25
Newcomb Ct. PE9: Stam 4F 7
Newcombe Way PE2: Pet 4H 23
New Cross Rd. PE9: Stam 4F 7
NEW ENGLAND 5G 13
NEW FLETTON 5H 19
Newgates PE9: Stam 4G 7
Newham Rd. PE9: Stam 2E 7
Newhaven Est. Mobile Home Pk.
   PE7: Whit 2B 30
New Hunting Ct. PE3: Pet 3G 19
   (off Thorpe Rd.)
New Lakeside PE7: Pet 6D 24
Newlands Rd. PE7: Whit 1F 31

Newmarket Cl. PE1: Pet 5B 14
New Meadow Drove
   PE7: Far 5D 26
New Rd. PE1: Pet 3D 4 (3B 20)
   PE2: Pet 5G 19
   (Earl Spencer Ct.)
   PE2: Pet 3A 24
   (Mill Cres., not continuous)
   PE6: Eye 1H 15
   PE7: Whit 4D 30
New Row PE6: Deep J 4E 9
New St. PE9: Stam 3G 7
Newton Ct. PE4: Pet 2H 13
Newton Way PE1: Pet 3D 20
NEWTOWN 5H 7
MINOR INJURIES UNIT (PETERBOROUGH)
   . . . . .3G 19
Nicholas Taylor Gdns. PE3: Pet 1B 18
Nicholls Av. PE3: Pet 2G 19
Nightingale Ct. PE4: Pet 1A 14
Nightingale Dr. PE7: Yax 3D 28
Nightingales PE6: Mkt D 3D 8
Norburn PE3: Pet 3D 12
Norfolk Sq. PE9: Stam 3F 7
Norfolk St. PE1: Pet 1H 19
Norham Ct. PE2: Pet 2G 27
Norman Cl. PE7: Whit 2D 30
NORMAN CROSS 6A 28
Norman Cross Gallery 6A 28
Normangate PE5: Ail 3B 16
Norman Rd. PE1: Pet 1C 20
Normanton Rd. PE1: Pet 4D 14
North Bank PE1: Pet 5G 5 (4C 20)
Nth. Bank Rd. PE1: Pet 2H 5 (2D 20)
NORTHBOROUGH 6F 9
Northey Rd. PE6: Pet 2H 21
North Fen Rd. PE6: Glin 1A 10
Northfield Rd. PE1: Pet 4H 13
   PE6: Mkt D 1B 8
NORTHFIELDS 2G 7
Northfields Ct. PE9: Stam 3G 7
Northfields Ind. Est.
   PE6: Mkt D 1D 8
Northgate PE7: Whit 2C 30
Northgate Cl. PE7: Whit 2C 30
Northminster PE1: Pet 2D 4 (2A 20)
Northminster Rd. PE1: Pet . . .2D 4 (2A 20)
North St. PE1: Pet 3C 4 (3A 20)
   PE2: Pet 5C 20
   PE9: Stam 4F 7
North Ter. PE1: Pet 5E 15
Northumberland Av.
   PE9: Stam 3E 7
Norton Rd. PE1: Pet 5H 13
Norwood La. PE4: Pet 1B 14
   PE6: Pet 1C 14
Norwood La. Cvn. Pk.
   PE4: Pet 1B 14
Nottingham Way PE1: Pet 5C 14
Nursery Cl. PE1: Pet 1A 20
Nursery Gdns. PE7: Whit 4E 31
Nursery La. PE1: Pet 4H 5 (3D 20)

O

Oak Av. PE1: Pet 5D 24
Oak Ct. PE7: Yax 3G 29
Oakdale Av. PE2: Pet 2D 26
Oakfields PE3: Pet 3C 18
Oak Gro. PE6: Mkt D 3C 8
Oaklands PE1: Pet 1B 20
Oakleaf Rd. PE1: Pet 5C 14
Oakleigh Dr. PE2: Pet 1F 25
Oak Rd. PE6: Glin 1A 10
   PE9: Stam 2B 6
Oaktree Ct. PE7: Yax 4D 28
Oak Vw. PE3: Pet 3B 18
Oban Cl. PE9: Stam 3C 6
Oban Dr. PE2: Pet 3G 23
Occupation Rd. PE1: Pet 5G 13

Odecroft PE3: Pet 4E 13
Odin Cl. PE7: Whit 2D 30
Old Bailey Rd. PE7: Pet 1C 28
Old Barn Pas. PE9: Stam 4F 7
   (off Castle St.)
   PE2: Pet 2C 12
Old Court M. PE1: Pet 6A 14
Old Crown La. PE7: Whit 3C 30
Oldeamere Way PE7: Whit 4E 31
Oldfield Gdns. PE7: Whit 2C 30
OLD FLETTON 6A 20
Old North Rd. PE8: W New 6A 16
Old Pond La. PE5: Cas 3C 16
Old Priory Farm
   PE6: Deep J 4G 9
Old School Mews, The PE7: Whit 3C 30
   (off Barr's St.)
Olive Mede PE7: Yax 3F 29
Olive Rd. PE1: Pet 4C 14
Oliver Rd. PE2: Pet 6D 24
Oliver St John Pl. PE3: Pet 3D 18
Orchard, The
   PE4: Pet 6E 11
   PE6: Mkt D 3C 8
Orchard Cl. PE3: Pet 2F 19
   PE6: Deep J 4E 9
   PE9: Stam 4F 7
Orchard Gro. PE6: Max 6A 8
Orchard M. PE2: Pet 5H 19
Orchard Rd. PE9: Stam 4F 7
Orchards, The PE2: Pet 3B 24
Orchard St. PE2: Pet 5H 19
   PE7: Whit 3C 30
Orchard Wlk. PE7: Yax 3F 29
Orchid Cl. PE7: Yax 2F 29
Orme Rd. PE3: Pet 1F 19
Orton Av. PE2: Pet 6G 19
ORTON BRIMBLES 2A 24
Orton Ent. Cen. PE2: Pet 4G 23
Ortongate Shop. Cen.
   PE2: Pet 4A 24
ORTON GOLDHAY 4C 24
ORTON LONGUEVILLE 2D 24
ORTON MALBORNE 3D 24
Orton Meadows Golf Course 1A 24
Orton Mere PE2: Pet 6D 18
Orton Mere Station
   Nene Valley Railway 6D 18
ORTON NORTHGATE 3F 23
Orton Parkway PE2: Pet 2H 23
ORTON SOUTHGATE 4A 24
ORTON WATERVILLE 3A 24
ORTON WISTOW 1G 23
Orwell Gro. PE4: Pet 2H 13
Osbourne Cl. PE4: Pet 2H 13
Osbourne Way
   PE6: Mkt D 3B 8
Osier Av. PE7: Pet 5F 25
Osprey PE2: Pet 5B 24
Osric Ct. PE1: Pet 6C 14
Oswald Rd. PE2: Pet 6F 19
Otago Cl. PE7: Whit 2E 31
Otago Rd. PE7: Whit 2E 31
Otterbrook PE2: Pet 2A 24
Oundle Rd.
   PE2: Pet 3E 23
   PE7: Alw, Ches 6A 22
   PE8: Elt 6A 22
Outfield PE3: Pet 2C 12
Overland M. PE2: Pet 1C 26
   (off Whittlesey Rd.)
Overstone Ct. PE3: Pet 5E 13
Overton Way PE2: Pet 3B 24
Owens Gdns. PE7: Whit 2B 30
Owl End Wlk. PE7: Yax 4D 28
Owl's End PE7: Whit 3D 30
Oxburgh Cl. PE2: Pet 2F 27
Oxclose PE3: Pet 3C 12
Oxford Gdns. PE7: Whit 3B 30
Oxford Rd. PE1: Pet 6H 13
   PE9: Stam 2E 7

Oxney Rd. PE1: Pet 6E 15
Oxney Road Cvn. Pk. PE1: Pet 6F 15
Oxney Rd. Ind. Est. PE1: Pet 5F 15

P

Paddock, The PE6: Mkt D 2B 8
PE9: Stam 4E 7
Paddocks, The PE4: Pet 4C 10
PE7: Whit 3D 30
PE9: Tin 6B 6
Padholme Rd. PE1: Pet 1F 5 (2B 20)
Padholme Rd. E. PE1: Pet 2D 20
Palace Gdns. PE2: Pet 6B 20
Palm Ct. PE1: Pet 3B 14
(not continuous)
Palmer Cl. PE7: Whit 4E 31
Palmer's Rd. PE1: Pet 6F 15
Palmerston Rd. PE2: Pet 6H 19
Panacea Ct. PE7: Pet 6D 20
Pandora Dr. PE2: Pet 3C 26
Pantiles, The PE1: Pet 1A 20
PE7: Whit 2C 30
Panton Cl. PE6: Deep J 3E 9
Papyrus Rd. PE4: Pet 5B 10
Parade, The PE2: Pet 1D 26
Paradise La. PE7: Whit 4C 30
Park Cl. PE7: Yax 4F 29
Park Cres. PE1: Pet 6B 14
Park Dr. PE6: Mkt D 3C 8
Parker Cl. PE9: Stam 2C 6
Park Est. PE6: Deep J 4F 9
PARK FARM 2F 27
Park Farm Cres. PE2: Pet 2F 27
Park Farm Rd. PE6: Mar 1H 17
Park Farm Way PE2: Pet 2F 27
Park Home Av. PE7: Pet 6F 25
Parkinson's La. PE7: Whit 4C 30
Park La. PE1: Pet 1H 5 (1C 20)
PE7: Whit 3B 30
PE9: Stam 5G 7
Parkodi Ct. PE1: Pet 1B 4
Park Rd. PE1: Pet 3C 4 (6A 14)
PE6: Deep J 4E 9
Parkside PE2: Pet 1D 24
Parkside Ter. PE9: Stam 3F 7
(off Recreation Ground Rd.)
Park St. PE2: Pet 6H 19
Park Ter. PE1: Pet 5A 14
Park Vw. PE9: Stam 5H 7
Parkview Flats PE1: Pet 1B 20
Parliament St. PE1: Pet 6H 13
PARNWELL 4F 15
Parnwell Local Cen. PE1: Pet 4F 15
Parnwell Way PE1: Pet 3F 15
Parry Cl. PE7: Pet 2H 25
Parslins, The PE6: Deep J 3G 9
Partridge Cl. PE7: Yax 3D 28
Partridge Gro. PE4: Pet 4C 10
Passport Office 3D 4 (3A 20)
PASTON 2A 14
Paston La. PE4: Pet 3F 13
Paston Parkway PE1: Pet 1A 14
PE4: Pet 4F 11
Paston Ridings PE4: Pet 2G 13
(not continuous)
Pasture, The PE6: Mkt D 2D 8
Pasture Dr. PE7: Pet 5D 24
Patterdale Dr. PE4: Pet 1A 14
Pauleys Ct. PE9: Stam 4G 7
(off St Leonard's St.)
Paulsgrove PE2: Pet 1H 23
Pawlett Cl. PE6: Deep J 3E 9
Paxton Rd. PE2: Pet 3H 23
Paynels PE2: Pet 4C 24
(not continuous)
Paynesholm PE4: Pet 2A 14
Peacock Sq. PE6: Mkt D 1C 8
Peacock Way PE3: Pet 3B 18
Peake Cl. PE2: Pet 1H 25

Peakirk Rd. PE6: Deep G, N'boro 5F 9
PE6: Glin 1B 10
Pearces Rd. PE6: Pet 6H 15
Pears Ho. PE1: Pet 4E 5
Pear Tree Cl. PE1: Pet 4G 13
Peartree Wlk. PE7: Yax 3G 29
Peckover Cl. PE2: Pet 2F 27
Peddars Way PE3: Pet 3C 18
Pelham Cl. PE3: Pet 3B 18
Pembroke Av. PE2: Pet 2B 24
Pembroke Gro. PE6: Glin 1B 10
Pembroke Rd. PE9: Stam 2E 7
Pendlebury Dr. PE6: Deep J 3E 9
Pendleton PE3: Pet 5D 12
Pennine Way PE4: Pet 1F 13
Pennington PE2: Pet 4A 24
Penrith Gro. PE4: Pet 1A 14
Pentlands, The PE4: Pet 1G 13
Pentney Cl. PE2: Pet 6C 20
Penwald Cl. PE6: Pea 1D 10
Penyale PE3: Pet 4C 18
Peppercorn Cl. PE1: Pet 5G 13
Percival St. PE1: Pet 3G 19
Peregrine St. PE7: Pet 6F 25
Pernys Cl. PE7: Pet 4F 25
Perth Rd. PE9: Stam 3B 6
PETERBOROUGH 4D 4 (3A 20)
Peterborough & District
Indoor Bowling Cen. . .2H 5 (2C 20)
Peterborough Arena 4G 23
Peterborough Bus. Pk. PE2: Pet 2F 23
Peterborough Bus Station . .3B 4 (3H 19)
Peterborough Cathedral . . .4D 4 (3A 20)
PETERBOROUGH CITY HOSPITAL . .1D 18
Peterborough City Mkt. PE1: Pet 3D 4
Peterborough City Rowing Club 4E 19
Peterborough Climbing Wall 1D 18
Peterborough Crematorium
PE6: Pet 2B 12
Peterborough Dr. PE6: Mar 2H 17
Peterborough Garden Pk. PE1: Pet . . .3D 14
Peterborough Greyhound Stadium
. . . . .6H 5 (4D 20)
Peterborough Milton Golf Course . . .3F 17
Peterborough Mus. 4B 4 (3H 19)
Peterborough (Nene Valley) Station
Nene Valley Railway 6B 4 (4H 19)
Peterborough Rd. PE1: Eye, Pet 3D 14
PE5: Ail, Cas, Sut 3A 16
PE6: Eye 3E 15
PE6: Mkt D 1A 8
PE7: Far 5C 26
PE7: Whit 3A 30
PETERBOROUGH SERVICE AREA 6F 23
Peterborough Speedway 3G 23
Peterborough Station (Rail)
. . . . .3A 4 (3H 19)
Peterborough Town Sports Club 1D 18
Peterborough United FC 5A 20
Peterborough Visitor Destination Cen.
. . . . .4C 4
(off Bridge St.)
Peterborough Webb Est. PE2: Pet . . .5F 19
Peterfield Rd. PE7: Pet 6D 24
Petergate PE9: Stam 5F 7
Peterhead Cl. PE2: Pet 2H 23
Peterhouse Cl. PE3: Pet 1A 4 (2G 19)
PE9: Stam 2F 7
Peters Ct. PE1: Pet 3D 4
Petworth Cl. PE6: Mkt D 3B 8
Peveril Rd. PE1: Pet 4H 13
Pheasant Gro. PE4: Pet 4C 10
Pheasant Way PE7: Yax 4D 28
Phillips Ct. PE9: Stam 5G 7
Phoenix Cl. PE2: Pet 1B 26
Phorpres Cl. PE7: Pet 4F 25
Phorpres Ct. PE2: Pet 1H 25
Phorpres Ho's. PE7: Pet 3H 25
Phorpres Way PE7: Pet 3G 25
Picketts Cl. PE7: Whit 3C 30
Pilton Cl. PE4: Pet 1H 13

Pinder Av. PE4: Pet 1A 14
Pine Cl. PE9: Stam 3B 6
Pine Tree Cl. PE1: Pet 3B 14
Pinewood Av. PE7: Whit 3D 30
Pinfold La. PE9: Stam 5G 7
(Old Great Nth. Rd.)
PE9: Stam 4H 7
(Priory Rd.)
Pingle Cl. PE7: Whit 3B 30
Pintail Gdns. PE7: Pet 1B 28
Pipe La. PE1: Pet 3E 5 (3B 20)
(not continuous)
Piper La. PE4: Pet 1B 14
Pipistrelle Ct. PE4: Pet 6E 11
Pittneys PE4: Pet 2H 13
Planet Ice 2C 12
Plough Cres. PE7: Whit 2C 30
Plough Rd. PE7: Whit 2B 30
Ploverly PE4: Pet 4E 11
Plover Rd. PE7: Whit 2E 31
Poles Ct. PE7: Whit 3C 30
Police Ho's. PE9: Stam 4F 7
(off Cliff Rd.)
Polls Yd. PE5: Cas 4D 16
Pomona Way PE2: Pet 3D 26
Ponsonby Dr. PE2: Pet 5E 19
Pooley Way PE7: Yax 3D 28
Pope Way PE1: Pet 3G 13
Poplar Av. PE1: Pet 3B 14
Popley Ct. PE1: Pet 6A 14
Poppy Cl. PE7: Yax 2G 29
Portchester Cl. PE2: Pet 2F 27
Portland Av. PE1: Pet 4H 13
Portland Pl. PE7: Whit 4D 30
Port La. PE5: Cas 4B 16
Portman Cl. PE3: Pet 1F 19
Potters Way PE1: Pet 6F 5 (4B 20)
Poulter Av. PE2: Pet 2D 26
Powerleague
Peterborough 2C 26
Pratt Av. PE4: Pet 1H 13
Precincts, The PE6: Mkt D 3D 8
Prestland PE6: Mkt D 2C 8
Priestgate PE1: Pet 4B 4 (3H 19)
Priestgate Ct. PE1: Pet 4B 4
Primrose Cl. PE1: Pet 3A 14
Primrose Dr. PE7: Yax 2F 29
Primroses PE6: Deep J 3E 9
Primrose Way PE9: Stam 2A 6
Prince's Gdns. PE9: Stam 1B 20
Princes Ga. PE1: Pet 1B 20
Princes Rd. PE2: Pet 6A 20
PE9: Stam 3F 7
Princess Gro. PE6: Mkt D 2D 8
Prince's St. PE1: Pet 1A 20
Priors Ga. PE4: Pet 5C 10
Priors Rd. PE7: Whit 3B 30
Priory Cl. PE6: Deep J 4G 9
Priory Gdns. PE7: Ches 4D 22
PE9: Stam 4H 7
Priory Rd. PE3: Pet 2G 19
PE9: Stam 4H 7
Proby Cl. PE7: Yax 4D 28
Prospect Pl. PE1: Pet 3E 21
Prospero Cl. PE2: Pet 1H 25
Providence Ga. PE2: Pet 2E 27
(off Coneygree Rd.)
Provident Pl. PE1: Pet 6F 15
Puffin La. PE7: Pet 1D 28
Pyecroft PE1: Pet 5B 14
Pyhill PE3: Pet 4D 12
(not continuous)

Q

Quantock Way PE4: Pet 2G 13
Queen Charlotte M. PE1: Pet 5A 14
Queens Av. PE6: Mkt D 3D 8
Queen's Dr. W. PE1: Pet 6A 14
Queen's Gdns. PE1: Pet 6A 14

QUEENSGATE 3B 4 (3A 20)
Queensgate Cen. PE1: Pet . . .3C 4 (3H 19)
Queen's Rd. PE2: Pet 6B 20
Queens St. PE9: Stam 3F 7
Queen St. PE1: Pet 4C 4 (3A 20)
  PE7: Whit .3C 30
  PE7: Yax 3F 29
Queens Wlk. PE2: Pet 1A 24
              (Chisenhale)
  PE2: Pet 5H 19
             (Orchard St.)
  PE9: Stam .4E 7
Quickset Drove PE7: Yax 5F 29
Quinion Cl. PE7: Whit 4E 31
Quinton Gth. PE3: Pet 6E 13

R

Radcliffe Cl. PE9: Stam 4F 7
Radcliffe Rd. PE9: Stam 3E 7
          (not continuous)
Raedwald Ct. PE1: Pet 1C 4 (2A 20)
Ragdale Cl. PE1: Pet 4E 15
Railworld 6B 4 (4H 19)
Rainbow Ct. PE4: Pet 2G 13
Raleigh Way PE3: Pet 5D 12
Ramsey Rd. PE7: Far, Pet 3G 27
  PE7: Whit .6C 30
Ramsey Way PE2: Pet 1E 27
Rangefield PE2: Pet 3A 24
Rasen Ct. PE1: Pet 1H 5 (2D 20)
Rathbone Cres. PE3: Pet . . .2A 4 (1A 20)
Ravel Cl. PE9: Stam 3D 6
RAVENSTHORPE 5E 13
Rayner Av. PE2: Pet 2E 27
Reach Drove PE7: Whit 5A 30
Recreation Ground Rd. PE9: Stam 3F 7
Rectors Way PE4: Pet 1H 13
Rectory Gdns. PE2: Pet 6B 20
  PE6: Glin .1A 10
Rectory La. PE6: Glin 1A 10
Redbridge PE4: Pet 3C 10
Redcot Gdns. PE9: Stam 3F 7
Redcot M. PE9: Stam 3F 7
Redgate Ct. PE1: Pet 4E 15
Red Lion Sq. PE9: Stam 4F 7
         (off All Saints St.)
Red Lion St. PE9: Stam 4F 7
           (off Broad St.)
Redmile Wlk. PE1: Pet 3C 14
Redshank Cl. PE7: Whit 1F 31
Redshank Way PE7: Pet 6E 25
Redwing Cl. PE2: Pet 6E 21
Redwood PE2: Pet 2D 24
Reed Cl. PE7: Pet 5E 25
Reedland Way PE7: Pet 6E 25
Reepham PE2: Pet 3H 23
Reeves Way PE1: Pet 1C 20
Reform St. PE9: Stam 4D 6
Regal Pl. PE2: Pet 5A 20
Regency Ho. PE1: Pet 1A 20
Regency Way PE3: Pet 4G 19
Regents Ct. PE1: Pet 1A 20
Regional Fitness & Swimming Cen., The
  . . . . .4F 5 (3B 20)
Reidy Gdns. PE7: Whit 2C 30
Renson Cl. PE4: Pet 3H 13
Reubens Yd. PE7: Whit 3C 30
         (off Low Cross)
Reynolds Ind. Est. PE1: Pet 1F 21
Rhine Av. PE2: Pet 5G 19
Ribes Cl. PE7: Pet 4F 25
Richardson Way PE7: Whit 3D 30
Richmond Av. PE4: Pet 1E 13
Ridge, The PE7: Pet 6F 25
Ridge Way PE2: Pet 5C 20
Rightwell E. PE3: Pet 6C 12
Rightwell W. PE3: Pet 6C 12
Riley Cl. PE7: Yax 3D 28

Ringstead Rd. PE4: Pet 2H 13
Ringwood PE3: Pet 2B 18
Ripon Cl. PE4: Pet 6D 10
Rippons Drove PE6: N'boro 6F 9
Risby PE3: Pet 3D 12
Riseholme PE2: Pet 4A 24
Rivendale PE4: Pet 1D 12
Riverbank Cl. PE6: Deep J 5F 9
Rivergate PE1: Pet 5D 4 (4A 20)
Rivergate Arc. PE1: Pet 5C 4 (4A 20)
River La. PE3: Pet 4A 4 (3H 19)
Riverside PE6: Deep G 5F 9
Riverside Cl. PE7: Whit 4C 30
Riverside Gdns. PE3: Pet 3F 19
         (not continuous)
Riverside Mead PE2: Pet 5B 20
Riverside Pl. PE9: Stam 5G 7
Robden Ct. PE2: Pet 6A 4
Robert Av. PE1: Pet 3H 13
ROBERT HORRELL MACMILLAN CENTRE
  . . . . .1D 18
Robert Rayner Cl. PE2: Pet 1F 25
Robin Cl. PE6: Mkt D 3D 8
Robin Hood Cl. PE3: Pet 3B 18
Robins Cl. PE2: Pet 5G 19
Roche Ter. PE6: Eye 1H 15
Rockbourne Pl. PE4: Pet 3G 13
Rockingham Cl. PE6: Mkt D 2A 8
Rockingham Gro. PE4: Pet 1E 13
Rockingham Rd. PE9: Stam 3C 6
Rock Rd. PE1: Pet 5H 13
  PE9: Stam .4E 7
Rock Ter. PE9: Stam 4F 7
Roden Way PE7: Pet 2H 25
Rolleston Gth. PE1: Pet 3C 14
Rolls Cl. PE7: Yax 2E 29
Roman Bank PE9: Stam 4D 6
Roman Cl. PE7: Whit 2E 31
Roman Gdns. PE7: Pet 3H 31
Roman Mill Gdns. PE9: Stam 3E 7
Romany Gdns. PE2: Pet 2D 26
Roma Rd. PE2: Pet 3C 26
Rookery, The PE2: Pet 6G 17
  PE7: Whit .4D 30
  PE7: Yax 4D 28
Rookery La. PE9: Tin 5A 6
Rose Av. PE2: Pet 6C 20
Rose Ct. PE7: Yax 2F 29
Rosedale Cl. PE4: Pet 6C 10
Rosehall Ct. PE1: Pet 1H 19
Rosemary Av. PE6: Mkt D 3D 8
Rosemary Gdns. PE1: Pet 3H 13
Rosewood Cl. PE7: Yax 4F 29
Ross Cl. PE2: Pet 2H 25
Ross Dr. PE9: Stam 2C 6
Rosyth Av. PE2: Pet 3H 23
Rothbart Way PE7: Pet 4E 25
Rotherby Gro. PE1: Pet 4E 15
Rothwell Way PE7: Pet 6E 19
Roundhouse Cl. PE1: Pet 2D 20
Routeco Bus. Pk. PE2: Pet 5G 23
Rowan Av. PE1: Pet 5C 14
Rowe Av. PE2: Pet 6F 19
Rowland Ct. PE4: Pet 3E 11
Rowledge Cl. PE4: Pet 2E 13
Roxburgh Rd. PE9: Stam 3D 6
Royce Cl. PE7: Yax 3E 29
Royce Rd. PE7: Pet 2D 20
  PE7: Alw 3E 23
Royle Cl. PE2: Pet 2E 25
Royston Av. PE2: Pet 1E 25
Rudd Cl. PE1: Pet 5G 5 (4C 20)
Rudyard Gro. PE4: Pet 6G 11
Ruelands Sq. PE4: Pet 6B 10
Rushmere PE2: Pet 1B 24
Rushton Av. PE4: Pet 6B 10
Russell M. PE1: Pet 2B 4 (2H 19)
Russell St. PE1: Pet 2A 4 (2H 19)
Ruster Way PE7: Pet 5D 24
Rustic Av. PE7: Pet 1B 28

Ruther Cl. PE2: Pet 5F 19
Rutland Bus. Pk. PE1: Pet 6F 15
Rutland Cl. PE1: Pet 3G 5
Rutland Rd. PE9: Stam 2H 7
Rutland Ter. PE9: Stam 5E 7
Rycroft Av. PE6: Deep J 3G 9
Rycroft Cl. PE6: Deep J 4G 9
Rydal Ct. PE4: Pet 6G 11
Ryhall Rd. PE9: Uffi 1H 7
Ryhall Road Ind. Est. PE9: Stam 2H 7

S

Sabre Way PE1: Pet 1F 21
Saddle Ct. PE4: Pet 3H 13
Saddlers Cl. PE6: Glin 1A 10
Saffron Cl. PE1: Pet 6A 14
Saffron Dr. PE7: Pet 1B 28
Sage's La. PE4: Pet 2E 13
St Alban's Dr. PE6: Eye 2H 15
St Andrew's Pl. PE7: Whit 4C 30
St Audrey Cl. PE2: Pet 1D 26
St Augustines Wlk. PE2: Pet 5G 19
St Bee's Dr. PE6: Eye 2G 15
St Benedicts Cl. PE6: Glin 1B 10
St Benet's Gdns. PE6: Eye 1H 15
St Botolph La. PE2: Pet 1E 25
St Clement's PE9: Stam 4F 7
St Davids Sq. PE1: Pet 4D 20
St Edmunds Ct. PE7: Pet 5F 25
St Edmunds Wlk. PE7: Pet 5F 25
St George Av. PE2: Pet 1E 27
St Georges Av. PE9: Stam 3H 7
St George's Sq. PE9: Stam 4G 7
St George's Pl. PE9: Stam 4G 7
St Guthlac Av. PE6: Mkt D 3B 8
St Hughes Cl. PE1: Pet 1C 20
St James Av. PE1: Pet 4H 13
St James M. PE6: Deep J 4E 9
St Johns Cl. PE3: Pet 3G 19
St Johns La. PE9: Stam 4F 7
St John's Rd. PE2: Pet 6B 20
St Johns St. PE1: Pet 4E 5 (3B 20)
  PE9: Stam .4F 7
St John's Ter. PE9: Stam 4F 7
St Judes Cl. PE3: Pet 1E 19
St Katherines M. PE7: Pet 5E 25
St Kyneburgha Cl. PE5: Cas 3C 16
St Leonard's Priory 4H 7
St Leonard's St. PE9: Stam 4G 7
St Margaret's Pl. PE2: Pet 1H 25
St Margaret's Rd. PE2: Pet 1H 25
St Mark's St. PE1: Pet 1C 4 (2A 20)
St Martin's Cl. PE9: Stam 5G 7
St Martin's M. PE1: Pet 6A 14
St Martin's St. PE1: Pet 6H 13
St Marys Cl. PE1: Pet 1B 20
  PE7: Far 5C 26
St Mary's Ct. PE1: Pet 3E 5 (3B 20)
St Marys Dr. PE2: Pet 3B 24
St Mary's Hill PE9: Stam 4G 7
St Mary's Ho. PE7: Whit 3C 30
St Mary's Pas. PE9: Stam 5G 7
         (off St Mary's Hill)
St Mary's Pl. PE9: Stam 4G 7
St Mary's St. PE7: Far 5C 26
  PE7: Whit .4C 30
  PE9: Stam .4F 7
St Michael's Ga. PE1: Pet 4F 15
St Michaels Wlk. PE6: Eye 1H 15
St Olave's Dr. PE6: Deep G 1H 15
St Paul's Rd. PE1: Pet 5G 13
St Paul's St. PE9: Stam 4G 7
St Pega's Rd. PE6: Pea 1C 10
St Peter's Arc. PE1: Pet 4C 4 (3A 20)
St Peter's Hill PE9: Stam 5F 7
St Peter's Rd. PE1: Pet 4D 4 (3A 20)
St Peter's St. PE9: Stam 5F 7
St Peters Ter. PE9: Stam 5E 7
St Peter's Va. PE9: Stam 5F 7

St Peters Wlk.—Stokesay Ct.

St Peters Wlk. PE7: Yax 3F **29**
St Vincent's Cl. PE6: Deep J 3E **9**
Salaam Ct. PE1: Pet 1H **19**
Salisbury Rd. PE4: Pet 6D **10**
Salix Rd. PE7: Pet 5D **24**
Sallows Rd. PE1: Pet 5B **14**
Saltersgate PE1: Pet 4F **15**
Saltmarsh PE2: Pet 3E **25**
Samworths Cl. PE5: Cas 3D **16**
Sanderlings, The PE6: Pea 1D **10**
Sandford PE3: Pet 6D **12**
Sandhurst Rd. PE7: Pet 6E **25**
Sandpiper Cl. PE7: Whit 2F **31**
Sandpiper Dr. PE2: Pet 1E **27**
Sandringham Cl. PE9: Stam 2F **7**
Sandringham Rd. PE4: Pet 3E **13**
Sandringham Way PE6: Mkt D 3B **8**
Sapperton PE4: Pet 3D **10**
Saracen Way PE1: Pet 1F **21**
Sargents Ct. PE9: Stam 3E **7**
Saturn Dr. PE2: Pet 3D **26**
Saunders Cl. PE2: Pet 5F **19**
Saville Rd. PE3: Pet 6F **13**
Saville Rd. Ind. Est. PE3: Pet 6F **13**
Saxby Gdns. PE1: Pet 3C **14**
Saxonbury Way PE2: Pet 1H **25**
Saxon Ct. PE9: Stam 5G **7**
Saxon Rd. PE1: Pet 1G **5** (2C **20**)
PE7: Whit 3A **30**
Sayer Ct. PE2: Pet 5B **24**
Scaldgate PE7: Whit 4D **30**
Scaldgate Ct. PE7: Whit 4D **30**
Scalford Dr. PE1: Pet 3C **14**
School Cl. PE3: Pet 6C **12**
School La. PE6: Glin 1A **10**
Scotendon PE2: Pet 4A **24**
Scotgate PE9: Stam 4F **7**
Scotgate M. *PE9: Stam* *4F* ***7***
(off Scotgate)
Scotney St. PE1: Pet 4F **13**
Scott Cl. PE2: Pet 1E **27**
Scott Dr. PE7: Yax 4D **28**
Scotts Rd. PE6: Glin 1B **10**
Searjeant St. PE1: Pet 6G **13**
Searles Ct. PE7: Whit 2C **30**
Searle Wlk. PE2: Pet 5G **19**
Seaton Cl. PE7: Yax 3D **28**
Seaton Rd. PE9: Stam 5F **7**
Sebrights Way PE3: Pet 2B **18**
Second Drift PE9: Wot 6F **7**
Second Drove PE1: Pet 4D **20**
Second Drove Ind. Est. PE1: Pet 4D **20**
Sellers Grange PE2: Pet 3D **24**
Selwyn Rd. PE9: Stam 2E **7**
Serlby Gdns. PE3: Pet 2D **18**
(not continuous)
Serpentine, The PE7: Pet 4F **25**
Serpentine Grn. Shop. Cen., The
PE7: Pet .5G **25**
Setchfield Pl. PE2: Pet 6H **19**
Sevenacres PE2: Pet 3A **24**
Severn Cl. PE4: Pet 2G **13**
Sewell Cl. PE6: Deep J 3F **9**
Seymour Pl. PE4: Pet 2B **14**
Shackleton Cl. PE6: Mkt D 1C **8**
Shackleton Way PE7: Yax 4D **28**
Shakespeare Av. PE1: Pet 4H **13**
Shamrock Cl. PE2: Pet 6D **20**
Sharma Leas PE4: Pet 6C **10**
Sharnbrook Av. PE7: Pet 6E **25**
Shearwater PE2: Pet 6H **17**
(not continuous)
Sheep Mkt. PE9: Stam 4F **7**
Sheepwalk PE4: Pet 2A **14**
Sheldrick Wlk. PE4: Pet 5C **10**
Shelley Cl. PE1: Pet 3G **13**
PE9: Stam 3C **6**
Shelton Rd. PE2: Pet 1D **26**
Shepherds Cl. PE4: Pet 5E **11**
Sherborne Rd. PE1: Pet 5D **14**
Sheridan Rd. PE1: Pet 3H **13**
Sheringham Way PE2: Pet 1E **25**
Sherwood Av. PE2: Pet 6H **19**
Sherwood Cl. PE9: Stam 4D **6**
Shipton Gro. PE7: Pet 1H **25**
Shire Gro. PE1: Pet 6C **14**
Shore Vw. PE7: Pet 5D **24**
Shortacres Rd. PE2: Pet 6H **19**
Short Drove PE6: N'boro 6G **9**
Shortfen PE2: Pet 3E **25**
Showcase Cinema
Peterborough 3H 5 (3D 20)
Shrewsbury Av. PE2: Pet 6F **19**
Shrewsbury Ct. PE2: Pet 6F **19**
Shropshire Pl. PE1: Pet 3F **5**
Shrub Rd. PE7: Pet 6E **25**
Silver Hill PE7: Pet 4F **25**
Silver La. *PE9: Stam* *4F* ***7***
(off High St.)
Silver St. PE2: Pet 6H **19**
Silverwood Rd. PE1: Pet 6H **13**
Silverwood Wlk. PE7: Yax 4G **29**
Silvester Rd. PE5: Cas 3C **16**
Singerfire Rd. PE5: Ail 3B **16**
Sissley PE2: Pet 5A **24**
Skaters Way PE4: Pet 5E **11**
Skye Cl. PE2: Pet 2G **23**
Skylarks Cl. PE7: Pet 4F **25**
Smallwood PE3: Pet 5D **12**
Smith Ho. PE1: Pet 4E **5**
Snoots Rd. PE7: Whit 3A **30**
Snowhills PE7: Yax 4E **29**
Snowley Pk. PE7: Whit 2A **30**
Sobrite Way PE4: Pet 2D **10**
Soke Parkway PE1: Pet 6D **12**
PE3: Pet .3B **18**
PE4: Pet .6D **12**
Somerby Cl. PE9: Stam 2F **7**
Somerby Gth. PE1: Pet 4D **14**
Somerville PE4: Pet 4C **10**
Somerville Rd. PE9: Stam 2E **7**
Sorbus Cl. PE7: Pet 4F **25**
Sorrel Cl. PE6: Deep J 2E **9**
PE7: Pet .1B **28**
PE9: Stam 3B **6**
Southdown Rd. PE7: Yax 4F **29**
Southfields Av. PE2: Pet 1D **26**
Southfields Dr. PE2: Pet 2D **26**
Southgate Pk. PE2: Pet 5G **23**
Southgate Way PE2: Pet 6G **23**
Southlands Av. PE1: Pet 5A **14**
Southoe Rd. PE7: Far 5D **26**
South Pde. PE3: Pet 2G **19**
South St. PE1: Pet 3E **5** (3B **20**)
PE2: Pet .6C **20**
South Vw. PE2: Pet 6H **19**
South Vw. Bus. Pk. PE9: Tin 6D **6**
South Vw. Rd. PE4: Pet 3F **13**
PE9: Stam *3G* ***7***
(off New Cross Rd.)
Southwell Av. PE4: Pet 5C **10**
Southwick Cl. PE4: Pet 2H **13**
Sovereign Pl. PE3: Pet 3G **19**
Spalding Rd. PE6: Deep J 3F **9**
Sparrow Rd. PE7: Pet 6F **25**
Speechley Rd. PE7: Yax 3F **29**
Speedwell Ct. PE6: Deep J 2E **9**
Spencer Av. PE2: Pet 2D **26**
Speyside Ct. PE2: Pet 3H **23**
Spinney, The PE6: Mkt D 3C **8**
Spinney Ho. PE7: Yax 4E **29**
Spinney Wlk. PE3: Pet 3C **18**
Spiros Rd. PE2: Pet 3E **27**
Splash La. PE5: Cas 5C **16**
Sprignall PE3: Pet 1B **18**
(not continuous)
Sprigs Rd. PE7: Pet 5D **24**
Spring Av. PE7: Pet 6D **24**
Spring Dr. PE7: Far 5B **26**
Springfield PE2: Pet 6A **20**
Springfield Rd. PE1: Pet 6H **13**
PE7: Yax .4F **29**
Springfields PE7: East 3H **31**
Spring Vw. PE2: Pet 6A **20**
Springwater Bus. Pk. PE7: Whit 5E **31**
Square, The PE1: Pet 2E **21**
Squires, The PE2: Pet 5H **19**
Squires Ga. PE4: Pet 6H **11**
Stables, The PE7: Whit 3C **30**
Stackyard, The PE2: Pet 2A **24**
Stafford Rd. PE7: Whit 4E **31**
Stagsden PE2: Pet 3B **24**
Stagshaw Dr. PE2: Pet 5B **20**
Stallebrass Cl. PE2: Pet 2E **27**
STAMFORD 4F 7
STAMFORD & RUTLAND HOSPITAL . . .3H 7
Stamford Arts Cen. *4G 7*
(off St Mary's St.)
Stamford Bus Station 4F 7
Stamford Cl. PE6: Mkt D 4C **8**
Stamford Indoor Bowling Cen. 4D 6
Stamford Leisure Pool 3H 7
Stamford Lodge Dr. PE6: Mar 1H **17**
Stamford Lodge Rd. PE6: Mar 1G **17**
Stamford Retail Pk. PE9: Stam 3H **7**
Stamford Rd. PE6: Mar 2A **12**
PE6: Mkt D, W Deep 4A **8**
Stamford Station (Rail) 5F 7
Stamford Tennis Club 3G 7
Stamford Theatre 4G 7
Stamford Wlk. PE9: Stam 4G **7**
Stamper St. PE3: Pet 2B **18**
Standish Ct. PE2: Pet 5F **19**
Stanford Wlk. PE3: Pet 1E **19**
STANGROUND 6C 20
Stanground Newt Ponds 3B 26
Stanground Sth. By-Pass
PE7: Far, Pet 4B **26**
Stanground Sports Cen. 2C 26
Stanground Wash Nature Reserve . . .5D 20
Stanham Way PE2: Far 3B **26**
Staniland Way PE4: Pet 4D **10**
Stanley Rd. PE1: Pet 1D **4** (2A **20**)
Stanley St. PE9: Stam 4G **7**
Stan Rowing Ct. PE2: Pet 6C **20**
Stanton Sq. PE7: Pet 5F **25**
Stanwick Ct. PE3: Pet 4A **4** (3H **19**)
Stapledon Rd. PE2: Pet 5H **23**
(not continuous)
Staplee Way PE1: Pet 5F **15**
Star Cl. PE1: Pet 2G **5** (2C **20**)
Star La. PE9: Stam 4G **7**
Star La. M. *PE9: Stam* *4G* ***7***
(off Star La.)
Star M. PE1: Pet 3G **5** (3C **20**)
Star Rd. PE1: Pet 4G **5** (3C **20**)
Stathern Rd. PE1: Pet 4D **14**
Station App. PE7: Yax 2G **29**
Station La. PE2: Pet 6A **18**
Station Rd. PE1: Pet 3A **4** (3H **19**)
PE5: Ail 5A **16**
PE7: Whit 3D **30**
PE7: Yax .2G **29**
PE9: Stam 5G **7**
(Welland M.)
PE9: Stam 5F **7**
(Wothorpe Rd.)
Staverton Rd. PE4: Pet 5C **10**
Stephenson Cl. PE7: Yax 3D **28**
Stephenson Ct. PE1: Pet 4E **5** (3B **20**)
Stephens Way PE6: Deep J 5G **9**
Stevern Way PE1: Pet 1F **21**
Steve Wooley Ct. PE2: Pet 3D **24**
Steward Way PE4: Pet 1A **14**
Stewartby Av. PE7: Pet 6E **25**
Steynings, The PE4: Pet 6E **11**
Still Cl. PE6: Mkt D 3C **8**
Stimpson Wlk. PE4: Pet 5D **10**
Stirling Rd. PE9: Stam 3D **6**
Stirling Way PE3: Pet 2C **12**
PE6: Mkt D 1C **8**
Stocks Hill PE5: Cas 4D **16**
Stokesay Ct. PE3: Pet 4D **18**

A-Z Peterborough 45

Stonald Av. PE7: Whit 2C **30**
STONALD FIELD 2A **30**
Stonald Rd. PE7: Whit 2A **30**
Stonebridge PE2: Pet 2E **25**
Stonebridge Lea PE2: Pet 2E **25**
Stonehouse Ct. PE2: Pet 1C **26**
Stonehouse Rd. PE7: Yax 4E **29**
Stone La. PE1: Pet 6H **13**
Stoneleigh Ct. PE3: Pet 3D **18**
Stonewort Av. PE7: Pet 6D **24**
Storers Wlk. PE7: East 4H **31**
Storey's Bar Rd. PE1: Pet 2F **21**
  PE6: Pet 2F **21**
Storrington Way PE4: Pet 6E **11**
Stowehill Rd. PE7: Pet 2H **13**
Stowgate Rd. PE6: Deep J 5H **9**
Straight Drove PE7: Far 6D **26**
Stratford Ct. PE1: Pet 4H **13**
Strawberry Av. PE3: Pet 6C **12**
Stuart Cl. PE2: Pet 1C **26**
Stuart Ct. PE1: Pet 1B **20**
Stuart Ho. PE1: Pet 3E **5**
Stukeley Cl. PE2: Pet 2D **26**
Stumpacre PE3: Pet 3C **12**
  (not continuous)
Sturrock Way PE3: Pet 3E **13**
Sudbury Ct. PE2: Pet 2F **27**
  PE7: Whit 2C **30**
SUE RYDER CARE (THORPE HALL HOSPICE)
  ....3E **19**
Suffolk Cl. PE3: Pet 3D **18**
Sugar Way PE2: Pet 5F **19**
Summerfield Rd. PE1: Pet 1H **19**
Summer Hill Cl. PE4: Pet 1F **13**
Sunderland Rd. PE6: Mkt D 1D **8**
Sunningdale PE2: Pet 1A **24**
Sunnybank PE9: Stam 4G **7**
  (off East St.)
Sunnymead PE4: Pet 3C **10**
Sussex Rd. PE9: Stam 3F **7**
Sutherland Way PE9: Stam 4D **6**
Sutton Ct. PE4: Pet 5D **10**
Suttons La. PE6: Deep G 5D **8**
Svenskaby PE2: Pet 1G **23**
Swain Ct. PE2: Pet 5H **19**
Swale Av. PE4: Pet 2G **13**
Swallow Cl. PE7: Whit 1F **31**
Swallowfield PE4: Pet 5D **10**
Swallow Wlk. PE6: Deep J 3E **9**
Swan Cl. PE7: Whit 2E **31**
Swan Ct. PE7: Pet 4G **25**
Swan Gdns. PE1: Pet 5E **15**
Swan Rd. PE7: Whit 2E **31**
Swanson Ho. PE9: Stam 3H **7**
Swanspool PE3: Pet 5D **12**
Sweetbriar La. PE4: Pet 3D **10**
Sweetbriars PE9: Stam 2A **6**
Sweet Cl. PE6: Deep J 3E **9**
Swift Cl. PE6: Deep J 4E **9**
Swine's Mdw. Rd. PE6: Mkt D 1E **9**
Sycamore Av. PE1: Pet 4B **14**
Sycamore Rd. PE7: Whit 4E **31**
Sydney Rd. PE2: Pet 2D **26**
Syers La. PE7: Whit 3C **30**
Symmington Cl. PE2: Pet 5H **19**

T

Tabor Ct. PE7: Pet 5F **25**
Tait Cl. PE1: Pet 6C **14**
Talbot Av. PE2: Pet 1F **25**
Talon Ct. PE7: Yax 2H **29**
Tanglewood PE4: Pet 3D **10**
Tanhouse PE2: Pet 2E **25**
Tansor Gth. PE3: Pet 6E **13**
Tantallon Ct. PE3: Pet 4D **18**
Tarragon Ct. PE1: Pet 1C **4** (2A **20**)
Tarrant PE4: Pet 3C **10**
Tasmans Cvn. Site PE6: Eye 2G **15**
Tattershall Dr. PE6: Mkt D 2B **8**

Taverners Rd. PE1: Pet 1H **19**
Teal Dr. PE7: Pet 1B **28**
Teal Rd. PE7: Whit 2E **31**
Teanby Ct. PE3: Pet 2B **18**
Teasel Way PE7: Pet 5F **25**
Teasles PE6: Deep J 2E **9**
Telford Dr. PE7: Yax 3D **28**
Temple Grange PE4: Pet 3D **10**
Tempestes Way PE2: Pet 4D **26**
Tennyson Rd. PE1: Pet 3H **13**
Tennyson Way PE9: Stam 3C **6**
Tenter Ct. PE9: Stam 5G **7**
  (off Wharf Rd.)
Tenter La. PE9: Stam 4G **7**
Tern Rd. PE7: Pet 5E **25**
Thackers Way PE6: Mkt D, Deep J ..3D **8**
The ....
  Names prefixed with 'The' for example
  'The Acorns' are indexed under the main
  name such as 'Acorns, The'
THE ORTHOPAEDICS AND SPINE
  SPECIALIST HOSPITAL 2C **12**
Third Drove PE1: Pet 3E **21**
Thirlmere Gdns. PE4: Pet 6G **11**
Thistle Cl. PE7: Yax 2G **29**
Thistle Dr. PE2: Pet 6C **20**
Thistlemoor Rd. PE1: Pet 4G **13**
Thomas Cl. PE3: Pet 2B **18**
Thomas Cook Bus. Pk., The
  PE3: Pet 1C **12**
Thompsons Ground PE7: Pet 4F **25**
Thorley Cres. PE2: Pet 5F **19**
Thornemead PE4: Pet 5F **11**
Thorney Rd. PE6: Eye 1H **15**
Thornham Way PE7: East 4H **31**
Thornleigh Dr. PE2: Pet 1E **25**
Thorn Rd. PE7: Pet 5E **25**
Thornton Cl. PE4: Pet 6G **11**
Thorofare La. PE7: Whit 3C **30**
Thorolds Way PE5: Cas 3B **16**
Thorpe Av. PE3: Pet 3E **19**
Thorpe Lea Rd. PE3: Pet ...4A **4** (3G **19**)
Thorpe Mdws. PE3: Pet 3F **19**
  (not continuous)
Thorpe Pk. Rd. PE3: Pet 3E **19**
Thorpe Rd. PE3: Pet 4A **4** (3A **18**)
  (not continuous)
Thorpe Wood PE3: Pet 4B **18**
Thorpe Wood Bus. Pk. PE3: Pet ..4A **18**
Thorpe Wood Health & Racquets Club
  ....4A **18**
Thorpe Wood Nature Reserve 4B **18**
Thorseby Cl. PE3: Pet 2C **18**
Threave Cl. PE3: Pet 5C **18**
Throep Wood Golf Course 5B **18**
Throstlenest PE7: Far 4C **26**
Thurlaston Cl. PE3: Pet 3D **18**
Thurning Av. PE2: Pet 1C **26**
Thuro Gro. PE2: Pet 4C **24**
Thursfield PE4: Pet 5E **11**
Thurston Ga. PE3: Pet 4C **18**
Thyme Av. PE6: Mkt D 3D **8**
Tilman Dr. PE7: Pet 3H **25**
Tilton Ct. PE1: Pet 3C **14**
Tintagel Ct. PE3: Pet 4D **18**
Tintern Ri. PE6: Eye 1G **15**
Tinus Av. PE7: Pet 6E **25**
TINWELL 6B **6**
Tinwell Rd. PE9: Stam 5C **6**
Tinwell Rd. La. PE9: Stam 5D **6**
Tirrington PE3: Pet 2C **18**
Titan Dr. PE1: Pet 3E **21**
Tithe Farm Pastures PE6: Lang ...1A **8**
Tiverton Rd. PE3: Pet 2E **19**
Tobias Gro. PE9: Stam 2A **6**
Toftland PE2: Pet 2E **25**
  (not continuous)
Tolethorpe Sq. PE9: Stam 3F **7**
TOLL BAR 1A **6**
Toll Bar PE9: Gt Cas 1A **6**
Tollgate PE3: Pet 6C **12**

Toll Ho. Rd. PE2: Pet 6E **19**
Toll Rd. PE7: Pet 2G **27**
Tom Lock Ct. PE1: Pet 1C **4** (1A **20**)
Toole Way PE6: Deep J 3H **9**
Topmoor Way PE4: Pet 2H **13**
Torkington Gdns. PE9: Stam 4F **7**
Torkington St. PE9: Stam 4D **6**
Torold Dr. PE7: Pet 5G **25**
Tourist Info. Cen.
  Peterborough 4C **4** (3A **20**)
  Stamford 4G **7**
Touthill Cl. PE1: Pet 3D **4** (3A **20**)
Tower Cl. PE7: Whit 2A **30**
Tower Ct. PE2: Pet 5H **19**
Tower St. PE2: Pet 5H **19**
Towler St. PE1: Pet 1C **4** (2A **20**)
TOWNGATE 2B **8**
Towngate E. PE6: Mkt D 2B **8**
Towngate W. PE6: Mkt D 2A **8**
Towning Cl. PE6: Deep J 3E **9**
Townsend Cl. PE1: Pet 1C **4** (2A **20**)
Trafalgar Ter. PE9: Stam 3G **7**
Trelowen Way PE7: Pet 2H **25**
Tresham Rd. PE2: Pet 4H **23**
Trienna PE2: Pet 2D **24**
Trinity Cl. PE1: Pet 5C **4** (4A **20**)
Trinity Rd. PE9: Stam 3E **7**
Trinity St. PE1: Pet 5B **4** (4H **19**)
  (not continuous)
Troon Cl. PE9: Stam 3C **6**
Troutbeck Cl. PE4: Pet 6H **11**
Truesdale PE9: Stam 4F **7**
  (off Scotgate)
TruGym
  Peterborough 3D **4**
Tuckers Ct. PE2: Pet 6C **20**
Tuckers Yd. PE2: Pet 1C **26**
Tudor Av. PE7: Pet 6E **25**
Tudor Cl. PE4: Pet 1G **13**
  PE7: Whit 2B **30**
Tudor Pl. PE6: Deep J 3G **9**
  PE7: Yax 4C **28**
Turners La. PE7: Whit 4C **30**
Turningtree Rd. PE7: Whit 6F **31**
Turnpike Rd. PE7: Pet 6D **24**
Turnpole Cl. PE9: Stam 1H **7**
Turnstone Way PE2: Pet 6D **20**
Twelvetree Av. PE4: Pet 4C **10**
Twitten, The PE7: Far 5C **26**
Two Pole Drove PE7: Far 5F **27**
Twyford Gdns. PE1: Pet 4D **14**
Tyesdale PE3: Pet 1C **18**
  (not continuous)
Tyghes Cl. PE6: Deep J 3G **9**
Tyler's M. PE7: Pet 6D **10**
Tyrrell Pk. PE1: Pet 3D **20**

U

Uffington Rd. PE9: Stam 4H **7**
Uldale Way PE4: Pet 1H **13**
Ullswater Av. PE4: Pet 1F **13**
Ulverston Cl. PE4: Pet 2B **14**
Underwood Cl. PE7: East 3H **31**
University Centre
  Peterborough 6B **14**
Uplands PE4: Pet 4E **11**
Upton Cl. PE2: Pet 2E **27**
  PE3: Pet 3C **18**

V

Vale Dr. PE7: Pet 6E **25**
Valence Rd. PE2: Pet 3B **24**
Valley Pk. Cen. PE2: Pet 6F **19**
Valley Pk. Rd. PE2: Pet 5F **19**
Valley Pk. Vw. PE2: Pet 5F **19**
  (off Valley Pk. Cen.)
Vancouver Way PE2: Pet 2H **25**

Vars Rd. PE7: Pet 5D 24
Vaughan Way PE2: Pet 5G 19
Vawser Cres. PE3: Pet 3G 19
Vence Cl. PE9: Stam 4E 7
Venus Way PE2: Pet 3D 26
Vere Rd. PE1: Pet 4H 13
Vergette Rd. PE6: Glin 1B 10
Vergette St. PE1: Pet 1F 5 (1B 20)
Vermont Gro. PE3: Pet 5A 4 (4G 19)
Vesta Cl. PE2: Pet 3D 26
Vetchfield PE2: Pet 2A 24
Vicarage Farm Rd.
    PE1: Pet 2D 24
Vicarage Gdns. PE7: Far 5C 26
Vicarage Way PE7: Yax 4D 28
Victoria Pl. PE1: Pet 1B 4 (1H 19)
Victoria Rd. PE9: Stam 3F 7
Victoria St. PE1: Pet 6A 14
    PE2: Pet 1H 25
Victory Av. PE7: Whit 2E 31
Viersen Platz PE1: Pet 4A 4 (4A 20)
    (not continuous)
Viking Ct. PE2: Pet 6D 20
Viking Way PE7: Whit 2D 30
Village, The PE2: Pet 1D 24
Village Farm Cl.
    PE5: Cas 3C 16
Vine St. PE9: Stam 4G 7
Vine Ter. PE7: Alw 3E 23
Vine Wlk. PE3: Pet 1E 19
Vineyard Rd. PE1: Pet 4E 5 (3B 20)
Viney Cl. PE1: Pet 6D 14
Vintners Cl. PE3: Pet 2F 19
Violeta Cres. PE2: Pet 3E 27
Violet Way PE7: Yax 5H 27
Virginia Cl. PE3: Pet 3C 18
Viscount Rd. PE2: Pet 1B 26
Vixen Cl. PE7: Yax 3F 29
Vokes St. PE2: Pet 5F 19
VP Square PE1: Pet 2F 21

W

Wade Pk. Av. PE6: Mkt D 4D 8
Wainman Rd. PE2: Pet 2F 25
Wainwright PE4: Pet 4C 10
Wakelyn Rd. PE7: Whit 3B 30
Wakerley Dr. PE2: Pet 6E 19
Wake Rd. PE1: Pet 3F 5 (3B 20)
Walcot Wlk. PE3: Pet 2C 18
Walcot Way PE9: Stam 3C 6
Walgrave PE2: Pet 4D 24
Walker Rd. PE6: Glin 2B 10
Walkers Way PE3: Pet 2B 10
Walnut Cl. PE7: Whit 3F 31
Walnut Gro. PE4: Pet 1F 13
Walnut M. PE3: Pet 3G 19
Walpole Ct. PE1: Pet 1A 4
Walsham Rd. PE7: Pet 1D 28
Walsingham Way PE6: Eye 1G 15
Waltham Cl. PE1: Pet 3D 14
Waltham Wlk. PE6: Eye 1H 15
WALTON 2E 13
Walton Pk. PE4: Pet 2E 13
Walton Rd. PE6: Mar 2A 12
Warbon Av. PE1: Pet 4H 13
Ward Cl. PE1: Pet 1F 5 (2B 20)
Wareley Rd. PE2: Pet 6A 4 (4H 19)
Warren Ct. PE7: Pet 5E 25
Warrenne Keep PE9: Stam 5F 7
    (off St Peter's Hill)
Warwick Rd. PE4: Pet 1E 13
Wasdale Gdns. PE4: Pet 1A 14
Wash La. PE7: Whit 2D 30
Water End PE3: Pet 3F 19
    PE7: Alw 2E 23
Water Furlong PE9: Stam 5E 7
Watergall PE3: Pet 3C 12
Watergate PE9: Stam 4G 7
    (off Gas La.)

Water La. PE2: Pet 1B 24
    PE5: Cas 4D 16
    PE6: Mar 2A 12
Waterloo Rd. PE1: Pet 6A 14
WATER NEWTON 6A 16
Watersend Rd. PE7: Pet 5E 25
Waterside Gdns. PE7: Whit 2C 30
Waterslade Rd. PE7: Yax 5C 28
Watersports Cen. 5G 17
Water St. PE9: Stam 5G 7
Waterton Cl. PE6: Deep J 4F 9
Waterton Way PE7: Pet 6D 24
Waterville Gdns. PE2: Pet 2B 24
Waterworks La. PE6: Glin 3A 10
Waterworth Rd. PE7: Hadd 6H 23
Watt Cl. PE4: Pet 1G 13
Waveney Gro. PE4: Pet 1G 13
Waverley Gdns. PE9: Stam 3D 6
Waverley Pl. PE9: Stam 3D 6
Wayford Cl. PE3: Pet 3C 18
Wayside Cres. PE7: Pet 6D 24
Weatherthorn PE2: Pet 2E 25
Weaver Cl. PE4: Pet 6H 11
Websters Cl. PE6: Glin 1B 10
Wedgwood Way PE3: Pet 2D 12
Weedon Cl. PE4: Pet 2H 13
Welbeck Way PE2: Pet 6F 19
Welbourne PE4: Pet 5E 11
Welland Cl. PE1: Pet 3A 14
Welland Ho. PE1: Pet 2F 5 (2B 20)
Welland M. PE9: Stam 5G 7
Welland Rd. PE1: Pet 4A 14
    PE6: Pet 3B 14
Welland Vw. PE9: Tin 6B 6
Welland Way PE6: Deep J 4F 9
Wellington La. PE9: Stam 4F 7
    (off High St.)
Wellington St. PE1: Pet 3E 5 (3B 20)
Wellington Way PE6: Mkt D 1C 8
Wells Cl. PE4: Pet 6D 10
Wells Ct. PE2: Pet 2D 26
    (Stukeley Cl.)
    PE2: Pet 1D 26
    (The Parade)
    PE9: Stam 5F 7
    (off Austin St.)
Welmore Rd. PE6: Glin 1B 10
Wenlock Way PE4: Pet 2G 13
Wentworth Lodge PE3: Pet 1E 19
Wentworth St. PE1: Pet 5C 4 (4A 20)
WERRINGTON 6E 11
Werrington Bri. Rd. PE6: Milk N 4F 11
Werrington Bus. Cen. PE4: Pet 6B 10
Werrington Cen. PE4: Pet 4E 11
Werrington Gro. PE4: Pet 1D 12
Werrington Industry Nth. PE4: Pet . . .5B 10
Werrington Industry Sth. PE4: Pet . . .1C 12
Werrington Leisure Cen. 5D 10
Werrington M. PE4: Pet 6E 11
Werrington Pk. Av. PE4: Pet 6E 11
Werrington Parkway PE4: Pet 5C 10
Wesleyan Rd. PE1: Pet 3A 14
Wessex Cl. PE2: Pet 6D 20
Westbourne Dr. PE6: Glin 1A 10
Westbourne Ho. PE1: Pet 2G 5
Westbrook Av. PE2: Pet 6H 19
Westbrook Pk. Cl. PE2: Pet 6H 19
Westbrook Pk. Rd. PE2: Pet 6H 19
Westcombe Sq. PE1: Pet 1E 21
West Delph PE7: Whit 1C 30
West End PE7: Whit 3B 30
    PE7: Yax 5D 28
West End Vs. PE9: Stam 4E 7
Westerley Cl. PE3: Pet 1E 19
Western Av. PE1: Pet 4A 14
Westfield Cl. PE7: Yax 4D 28
Westfield Rd. PE1: Pet 1F 19
    PE3: Pet 1F 19
    PE7: Yax 5D 28
Westgate PE1: Pet 3B 4 (3H 19)

Westhawe PE3: Pet 4B 12
West Lake Av. PE7: Pet 6D 24
Westminster Gdns. PE6: Eye 2G 15
Westminster Pl. PE7: Pet 6F 15
Westmoreland Gdns.
    PE1: Pet 3E 5 (3B 20)
West Pde. PE7: Pet 2F 19
Westside Health Club 4E 7
West Stonebridge PE2: Pet 2E 25
West St. PE9: Stam 5E 7
West St. Bus. Pk. PE9: Stam 4E 7
West St. Gdns. PE9: Stam 4E 7
West Water Cres. PE7: Pet 6E 25
WESTWOOD 6F 13
Westwood Pk. Cl. PE3: Pet 2E 19
Westwood Rd. PE3: Pet 2F 19
Wetherby Way PE1: Pet 1H 5 (2D 20)
Weymouth Way PE1: Pet 5D 14
Whalley St. PE1: Pet 1E 5 (2B 20)
Wharf Rd. PE2: Pet 6A 4 (5G 19)
    PE9: Stam 5G 7
Wharf Rd. Ind. Est.
    PE2: Pet 6A 4 (4G 19)
Wheatdole PE2: Pet 4C 24
Wheel Yd. PE1: Pet 4D 4 (3A 20)
Whetstone Ct. PE1: Pet 4E 15
Whiston Cl. PE4: Pet 1H 13
Whitacre PE1: Pet 5F 15
Whitby Av. PE4: Pet 1H 15
Whiteacres PE7: Whit 2D 30
Whitebeam Cl. PE7: Pet 4F 25
White Cross PE3: Pet 5D 12
Whitecross PE7: East 3H 31
Whitehead Drove PE1: Pet 3E 21
White Post Rd. Sth.
    PE6: Eye, Newb 1E 15
Whitewater PE2: Pet 1H 23
Whitley Way PE6: Mkt D 1D 8
Whitmore St. PE7: Whit 3C 30
Whitsed St. PE7: Pet 1F 5 (2B 20)
Whittington PE1: Pet 4E 15
WHITTLESEY 3C 30
Whittlesey Mus. 3C 30
Whittlesey Rd. PE2: Pet 6B 20
    PE7: Pet 1C 26
Whittlesey Station (Rail) 5E 31
Whitwell PE4: Pet 1A 14
Wicken Way PE3: Pet 5E 13
Wick Rd. PE7: Pet 5D 24
Wigmore Dr. PE2: Pet 2F 27
Wilberforce Rd. PE1: Pet 4H 13
Wild Boar Cl. PE7: Whit 4D 30
Wildlake PE2: Pet 2E 25
Wildlife Haven 5B 4 (4H 19)
Willan Ct. PE2: Pet 5H 19
Willesden Av. PE4: Pet 3F 13
William Ct. PE9: Stam 2E 7
William Nichols Ct. PE1: Pet 1B 20
    (off Huntly Gro.)
Williamson Av. PE3: Pet 2G 19
Willonholt PE3: Pet 5E 13
Willoughby Av. PE6: Mkt D 2D 8
Willoughby Ct. PE1: Pet 4E 15
Willoughby Rd. PE9: Stam 2G 7
Willow Av. PE1: Pet 4B 14
Willow Cl. PE7: Whit 3B 30
Willow Ga. PE1: Pet 5D 14
Willow Hall La. PE6: Pet 2H 21
Willow Holt PE7: Pet 4E 25
Willow Lodge PE2: Pet 6D 20
Willow Rd. PE7: Yax 3G 29
    PE9: Stam 2B 6
Willow Rd. Ind. Est. PE7: Yax 3G 29
Willows, The PE6: Glin 1B 10
Wilton Cl. PE3: Pet 1E 19
Wilton Dr. PE3: Pet 1E 19
Wimborne Dr. PE1: Pet 4E 15
Winchester Pl. PE3: Pet 3G 19
    (off Thorpe Rd.)
Winchester Way PE3: Pet 4G 19
Windermere Way PE4: Pet 6G 11

Windmill Cl. PE6: Deep J 3G 9
Windmill St. PE1: Pet 6H 13
   PE7: Whit 2C 30
Windmill Way PE9: Stam 4E 7
Windrush Dr. PE4: Pet 2H 13
Windsor Av. PE4: Pet 3E 13
Windsor Cl. PE9: Stam 2F 7
Windsor Dr. PE2: Pet 1D 26
Windsor Pl. PE7: Whit 4F 31
   PE6: Mkt D 3C 8
Windsor Rd. PE7: Yax 3F 29
Wingfield PE2: Pet 5B 24
Winslow Rd. PE3: Pet 2E 19
Winsor Cres. PE7: Pet 1A 28
Winston Way PE7: Far 5C 26
Winterton PE4: Pet 2A 14
Winterton Cl. PE9: Stam 3D 6
Winwick Pl. PE3: Pet 6E 13
Winyates PE2: Pet 4B 24
Wisteria Rd. PE7: Yax 5D 28
Wisteria Way PE4: Pet 6F 11
Wistow Way PE2: Pet 1G 23
Witham Cl. PE9: Stam 3G 7
Witham Way PE4: Pet 2H 13
Woad Ct. PE6: Eye 1H 15
Woburn Cl. PE3: Pet 4C 18
   PE6: Mkt D 3B 8
Wollaston Rd. PE3: Pet 5E 13
Wolseley Cl. PE7: Yax 3E 29
Woodbine M. PE1: Pet 1F 5 (2B 20)
Woodbine St. PE2: Pet 6A 20
Woodbyth Rd. PE1: Pet 5A 14

Woodcote Cl. PE1: Pet 4A 14
Woodcroft Cl. PE6: Mkt D 3B 8
Woodcroft Rd. PE6: Mar 2A 12
Woodfield Rd. PE3: Pet 2F 19
Woodhall Ri. PE4: Pet 3D 10
Woodhead Cl. PE9: Stam 2H 7
Woodhurst Rd. PE2: Pet 1D 26
Woodlands, The PE1: Pet 6D 14
WOODSTON .5G 19
Woodston Bus. Cen. PE2: Pet 1F 25
Woodston Ga. PE2: Pet 1F 25
Woodston Ind. Est. PE2: Pet 1G 25
Woodston Ponds Bird Sanctuary 4F 19
Woodston Reach PE2: Pet 6A 4 (4A 20)
Woodward Dr. PE4: Pet 6H 11
Woolfehill Rd. PE6: Eye 1F 15
Woolgard PE3: Pet 3C 18
Woolpack La. PE7: Whit 4C 30
Wootton Av. PE2: Pet 1H 25
Worcester Cres. PE9: Stam 3F 7
Wordsworth Cl. PE4: Pet 3G 13
Worsley PE2: Pet 3C 24
WOTHORPE 6G 7
Wothorpe M. PE9: Stam 5F 7
Wothorpe Pk. PE9: Wot 6F 7
Wothorpe Rd. PE9: Stam 5F 7
Wren Cl. PE6: Mkt D 3D 8
Wright Av. PE2: Pet 2E 27

Wroxton Ct. PE6: Eye 1G 15
Wulfric Sq. PE3: Pet 3E 13
Wycliffe Gro. PE4: Pet 4C 10
Wye Pl. PE4: Pet 2G 13
Wye Valley Rd.
   PE2: Pet 5G 19
Wykes, The PE7: Yax 6C 28
Wykes Rd. PE7: Yax 5D 28
Wykes Way PE7: Yax 6C 28
Wyman Way PE2: Pet 2B 24
Wyndham Pk. PE2: Pet 1H 23
Wype Rd. PE7: East, Whit 3H 31

Y

Yarwell Cl. PE2: Pet 6F 19
Yarwells Headland PE7: Whit 2B 30
Yarwells Wlk. PE7: Whit 2C 30
YAXLEY 3F 29
YAXLEY FEN 5H 29
Yeoman PE3: Pet 1E 19
Yew Tree Wlk. PE3: Pet 3C 18
York Rd. PE1: Pet 5H 13
   PE9: Stam .3F 7

Z

Zara Ct. PE9: Stam 3F 7
Zebra Cotts. PE9: Stam 4D 6

MIX
Paper from
responsible sources
FSC® C021017
www.fsc.org

Copyright of Geographers' A-Z Map Company Ltd.

No reproduction by any method whatsoever of any part of this publication is permitted without the prior consent of
the copyright owners.

The representation on the maps of a road, track or footpath is no evidence of the existence of a right of way.

SAFETY CAMERA INFORMATION

PocketGPSWorld.com's CamerAlert is a self-contained speed and red light camera warning system for
SatNavs and Android or Apple iOS smartphones/tablets. Visit www.cameralert.com to download.

Safety camera locations are publicised by the Safer Roads Partnership which operates them in order to encourage drivers to comply
with speed limits at these sites. It is the driver's absolute responsibility to be aware of and to adhere to speed limits at all times.

By showing this safety camera information it is the intention of Geographers' A-Z Map Company Ltd. to encourage
safe driving and greater awareness of speed limits and vehicle speed. Data accurate at time of printing.

Printed and bound in the United Kingdom by Gemini Press Ltd., Shoreham-by-Sea, West Sussex
Printed on materials from a sustainable source